FOR ORGANS, PIANOS & ELECTRONIC KEYBOARDS

E-Z PLAY TODAY

170

KENNY ROGERS
Greatest Hits

T0042524

CONTENTS

Lucille

Registration 2
Rhythm: Waltz

Words and Music by Roger Bowling
and Hal Bynum

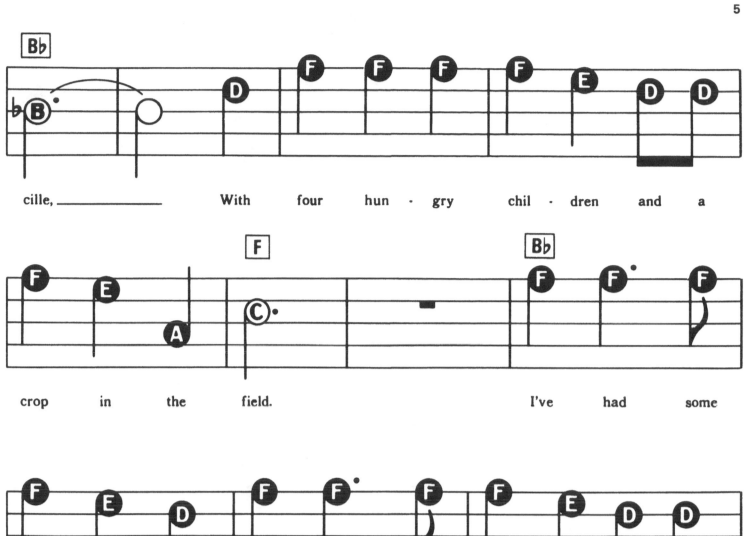

cille, _____ With four hun - gry chil - dren and a

crop in the field. I've had some

bad times,_____ lived through some sad times,_____ but

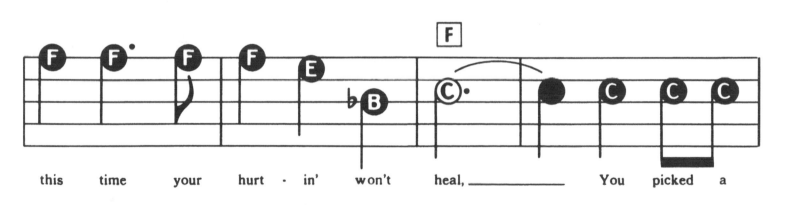

this time your hurt - in' won't heal, _____ You picked a

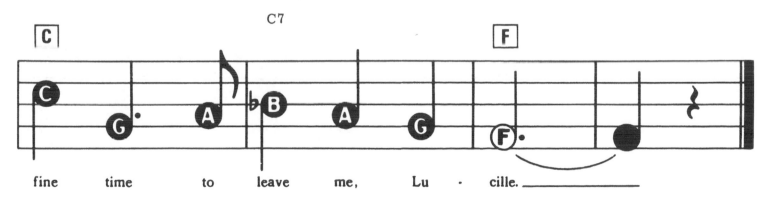

fine time to leave me, Lu - cille. _____

Through The Years

Words and Music by Steve Dorff
and Marty Panzer

Registration 4
Rhythm: Soft Rock or Ballad

I\
can't re - mem - ber when you were - n't\
can't re - mem - ber what I used to

there\
do When I did - n't care for\
Who I trust - ed Who I

an - y - one but you\
lis - tened to be - fore

I\
I

swear _____ we've been through ev - ery - thing there is Can't im - a - gine\
swear _____ you've taught me ev - ery - thing I know Can't im - a - gine

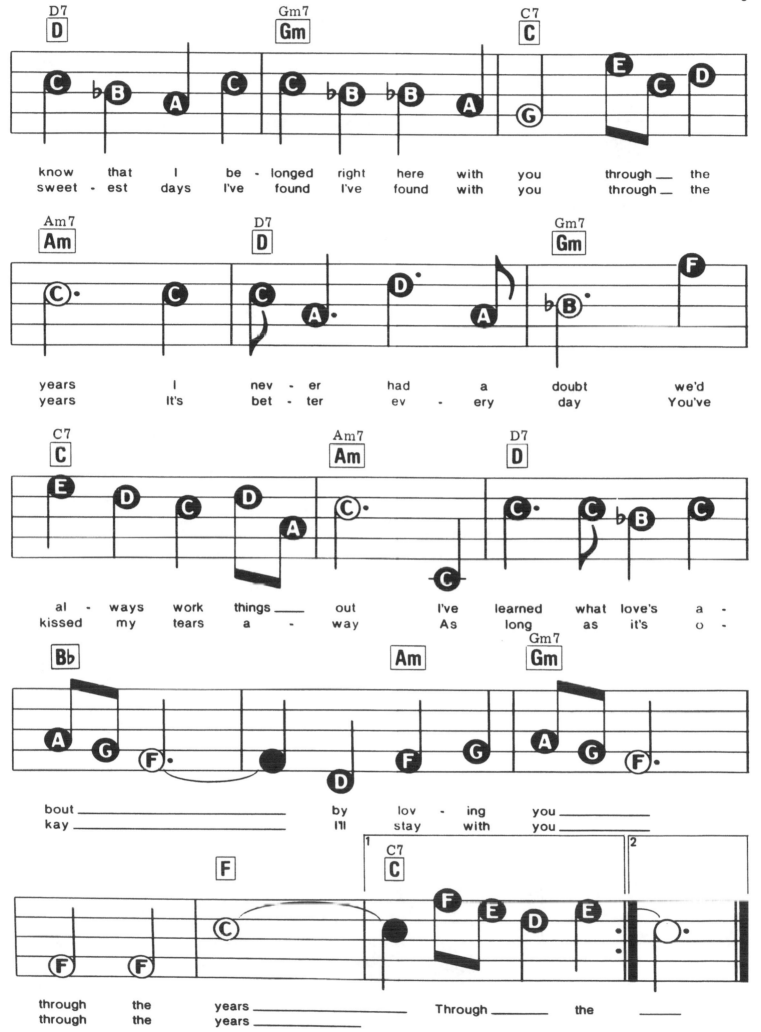

All I Ever Need Is You

Words and Music by
Jimmy Holiday and Eddie Reeves

Registration 3
Rhythm: March

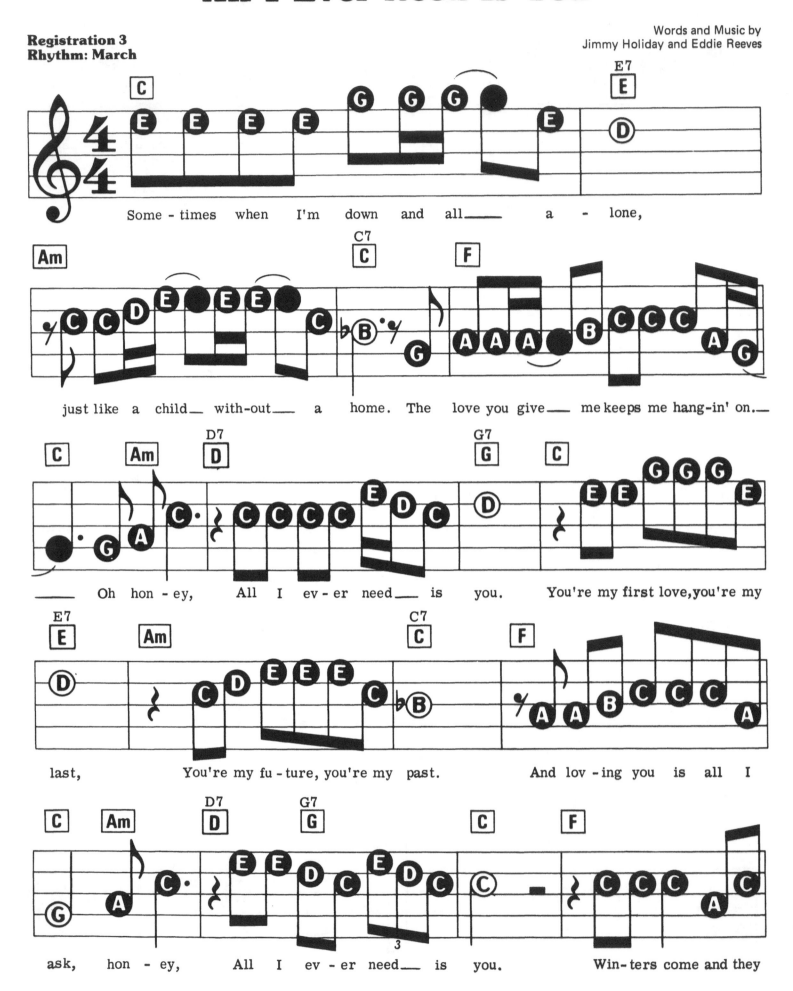

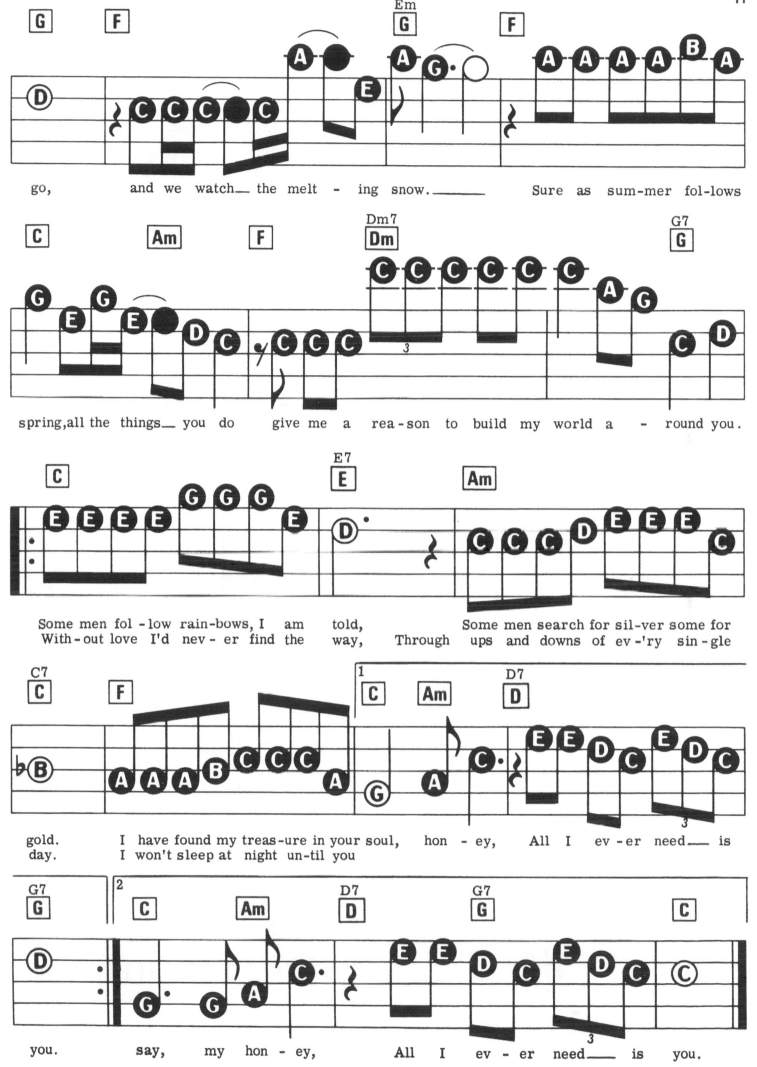

The Gambler

Registration 7
Rhythm: Country Western

Words and Music by Don Schlitz

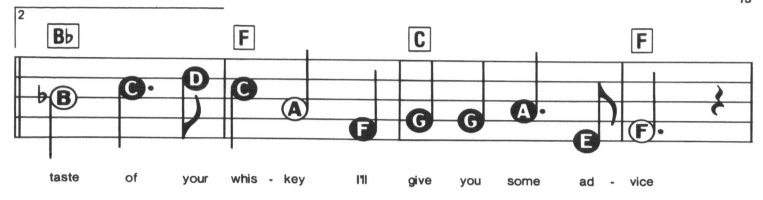

taste   of   your   whis - key   I'll   give   you   some   ad - vice

So   I   hand - ed   him   my   bot - tle   and   he

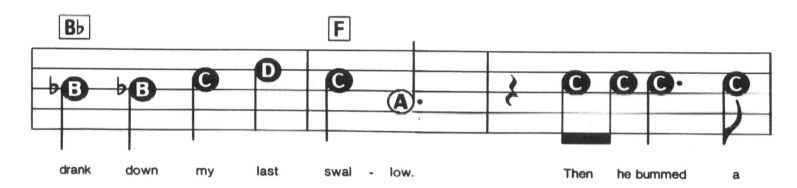

drank   down   my   last   swal - low.   Then   he bummed   a

cig - a - rette   and   asked   me   for   a   light   And   the

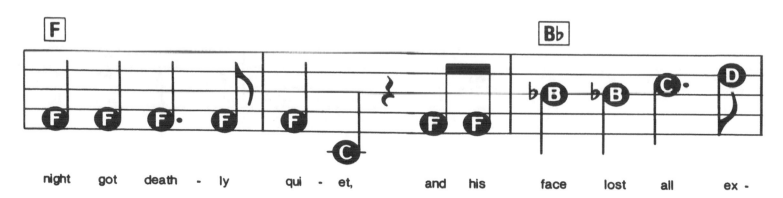

night   got   death - ly   qui - et,   and   his   face   lost   all   ex -

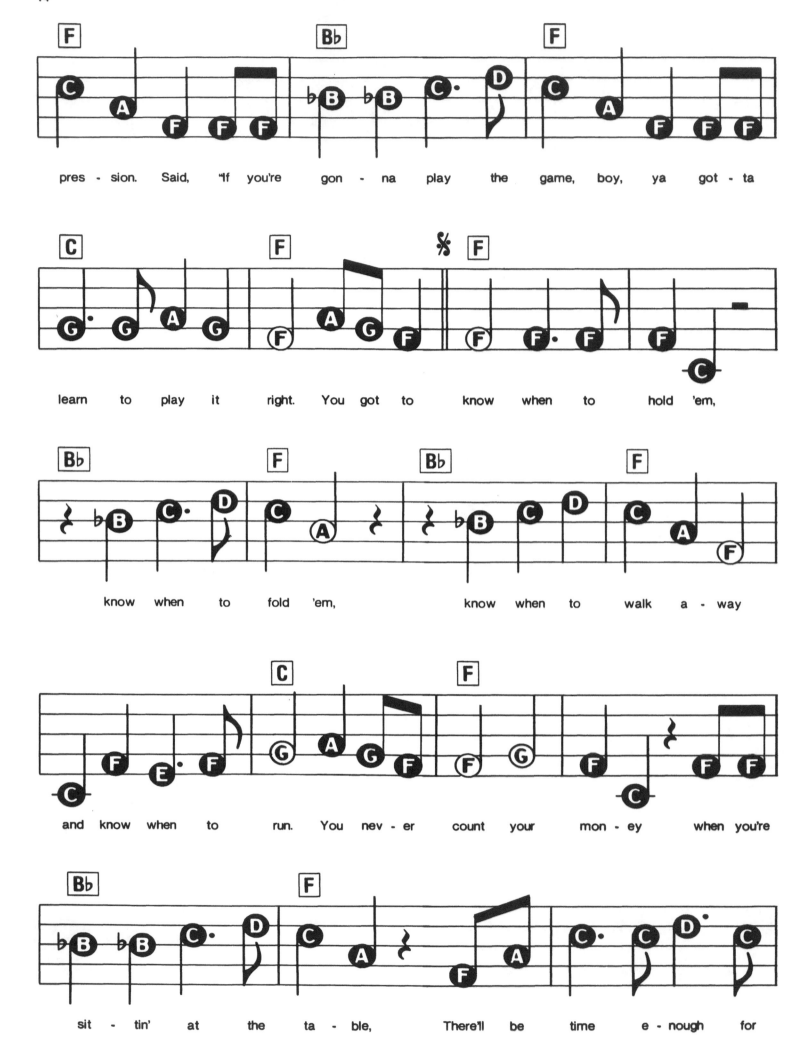

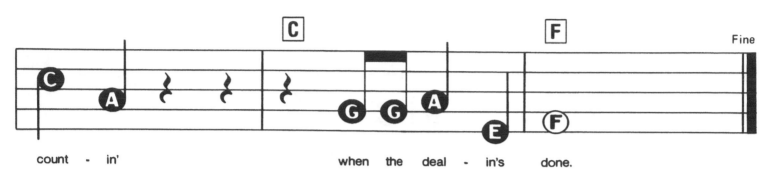

count - in'   when the deal - in's done.

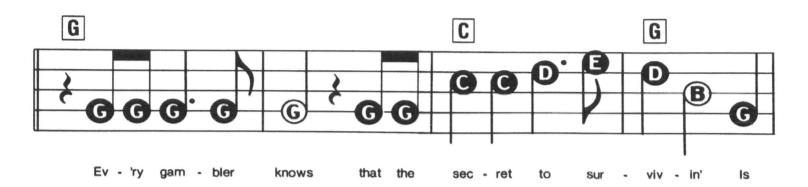

Ev - 'ry gam - bler   knows   that the   sec - ret   to   sur - viv - in'   Is

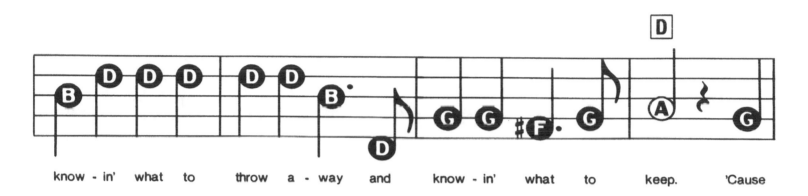

know - in' what to   throw a - way   and   know - in' what to   keep.   'Cause

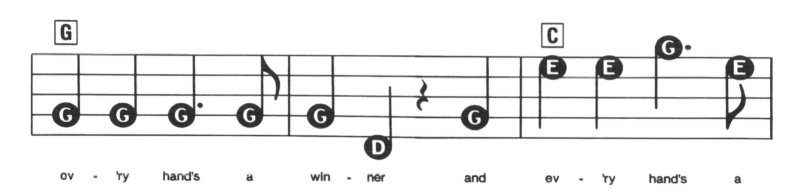

ev - 'ry hand's   a   win - ner   and   ev - 'ry hand's   a

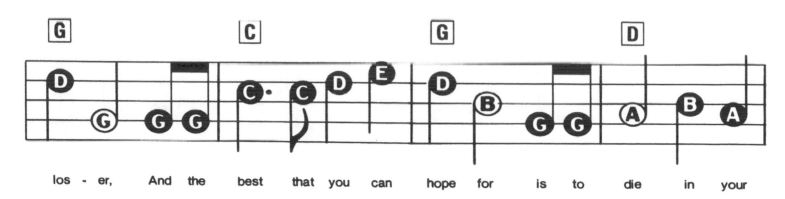

los - er,   And the   best   that you   can   hope   for   is   to   die   in   your

Without You In My Life

Registration 2
Rhythm: Ballad

Words and Music by Lionel Richie
and Thomas McClary

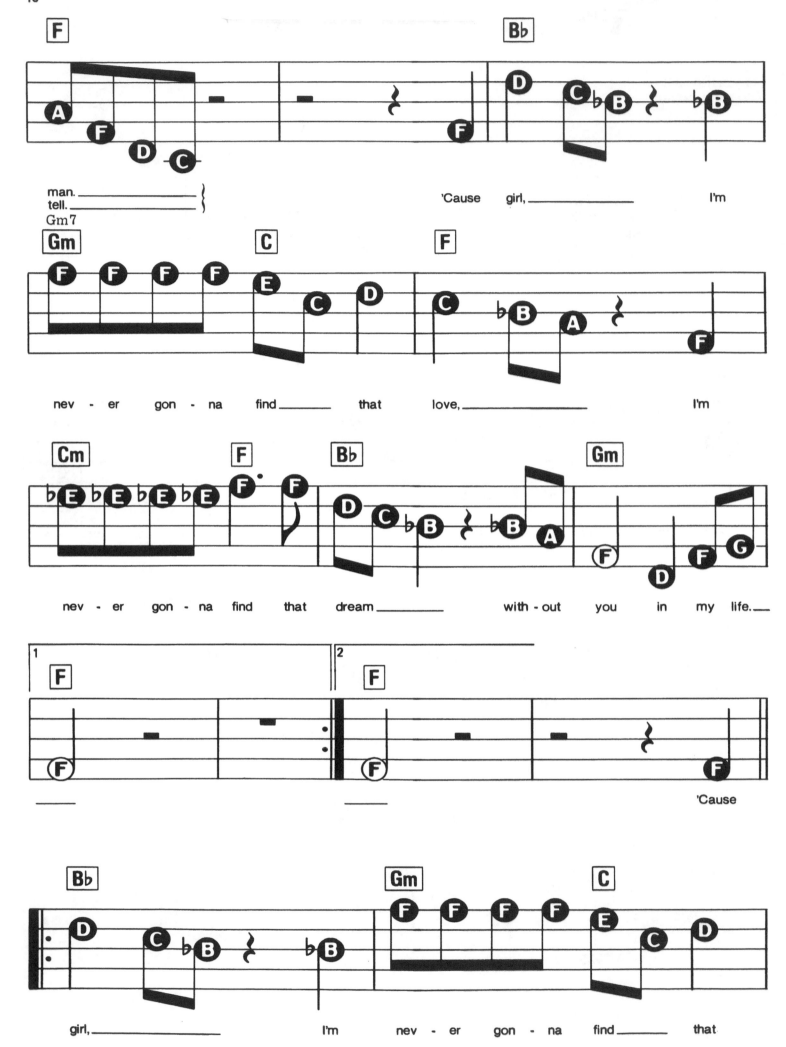

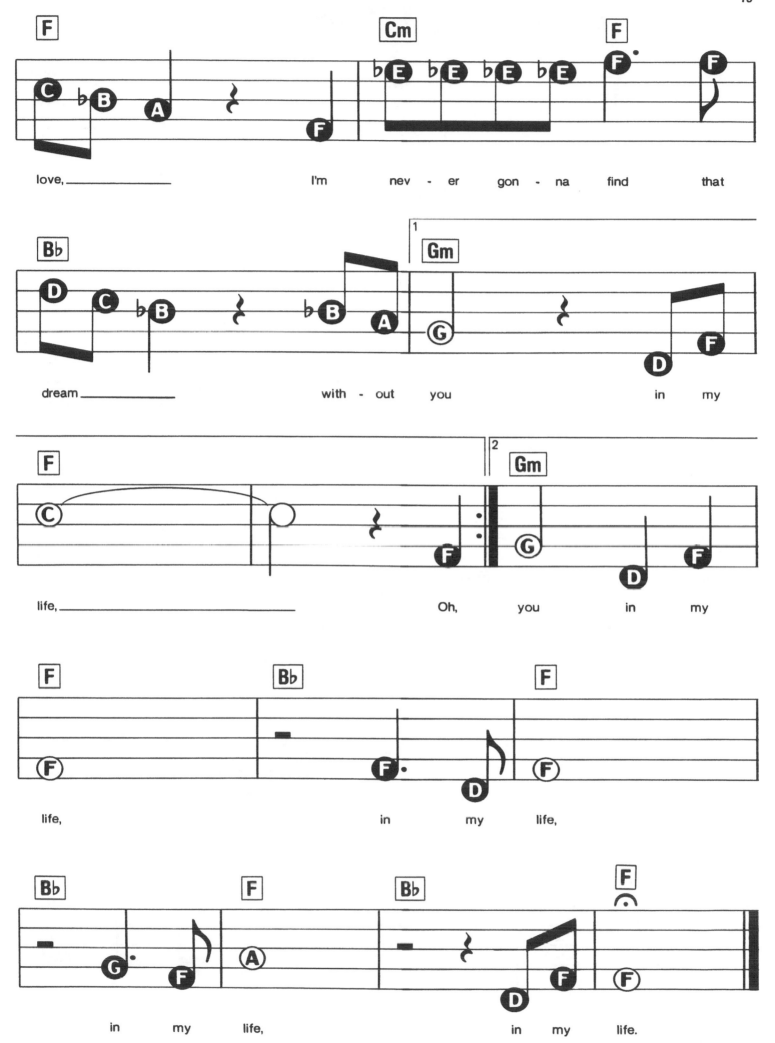

Coward Of The County

Registration 7
Rhythm: Country Western

Words and Music by Roger Bowling
and Billy Edd Wheeler

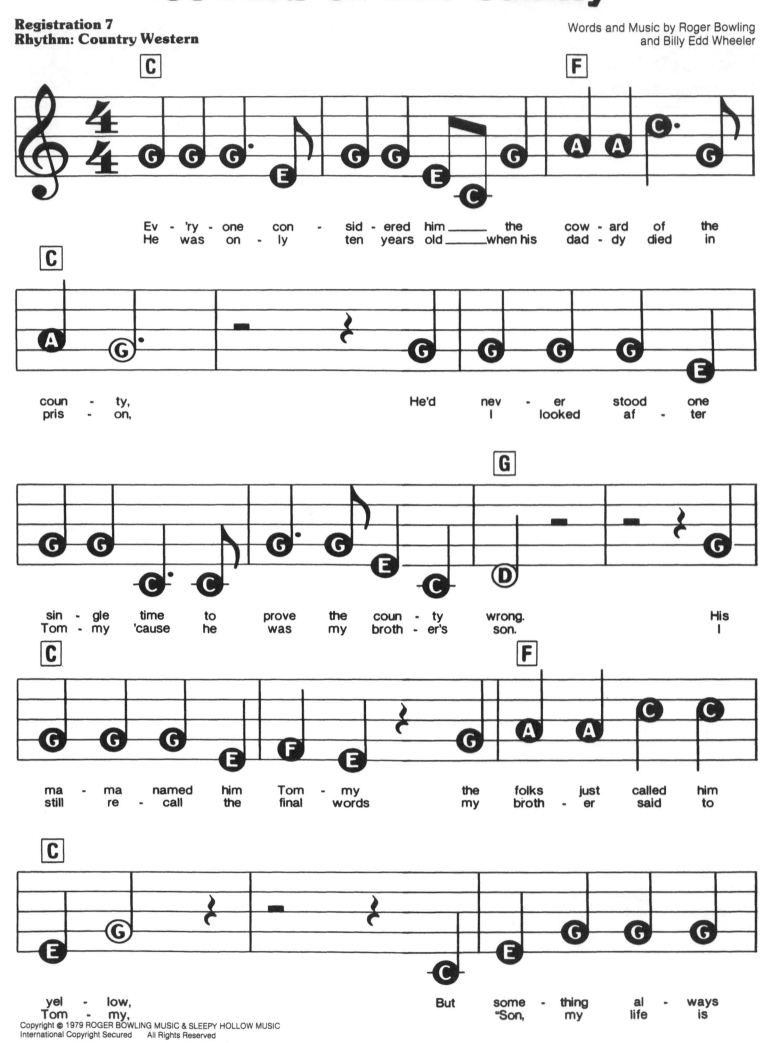

Ev - 'ry - one con - sid - ered him _____ the cow - ard of the
He was on - ly ten years old _____ when his dad - dy died in

coun - ty,
pris - on,
He'd nev - er stood one
I looked af - ter

sin - gle time to prove the coun - ty wrong. His
Tom - my 'cause he was my broth - er's son. I

ma - ma named him Tom - my the folks just called him
still re - call the final words my broth - er said to

yel - low,
Tom - my,
But some - thing al - ways
"Son, my life is

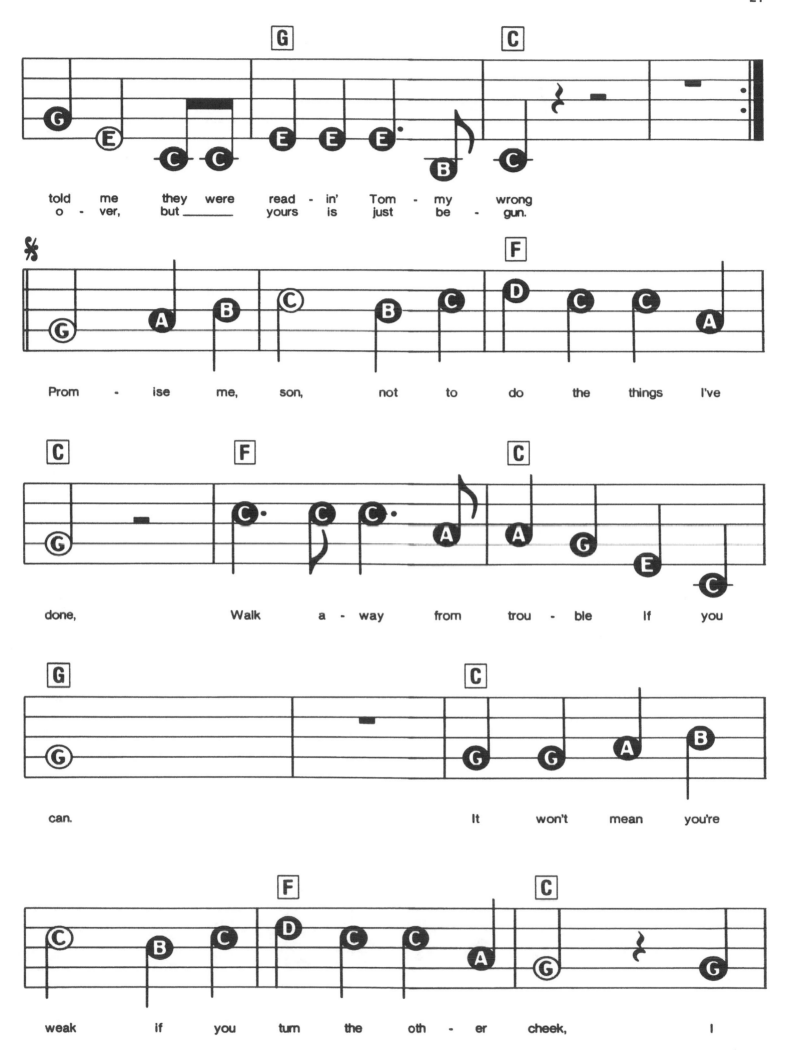

told me they were read - in' Tom - my wrong
o - ver, but _____ yours is just be - gun.

Prom - ise me, son, not to do the things I've

done, Walk a - way from trou - ble If you

can. It won't mean you're

weak if you turn the oth - er cheek, I

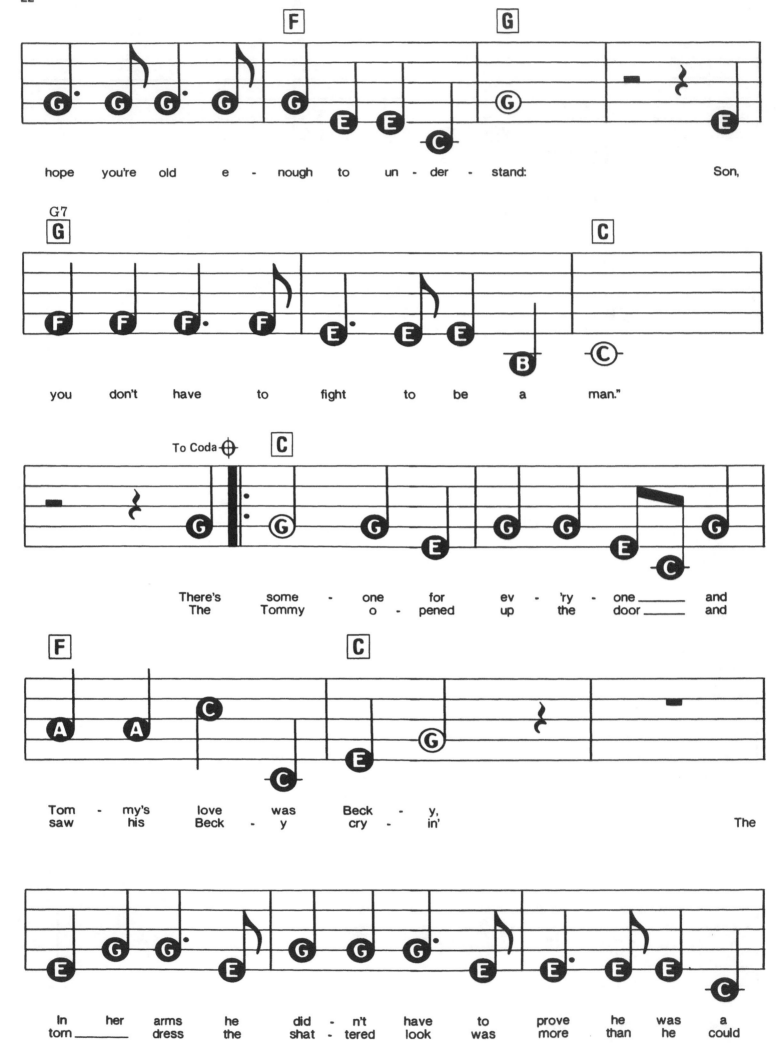

23

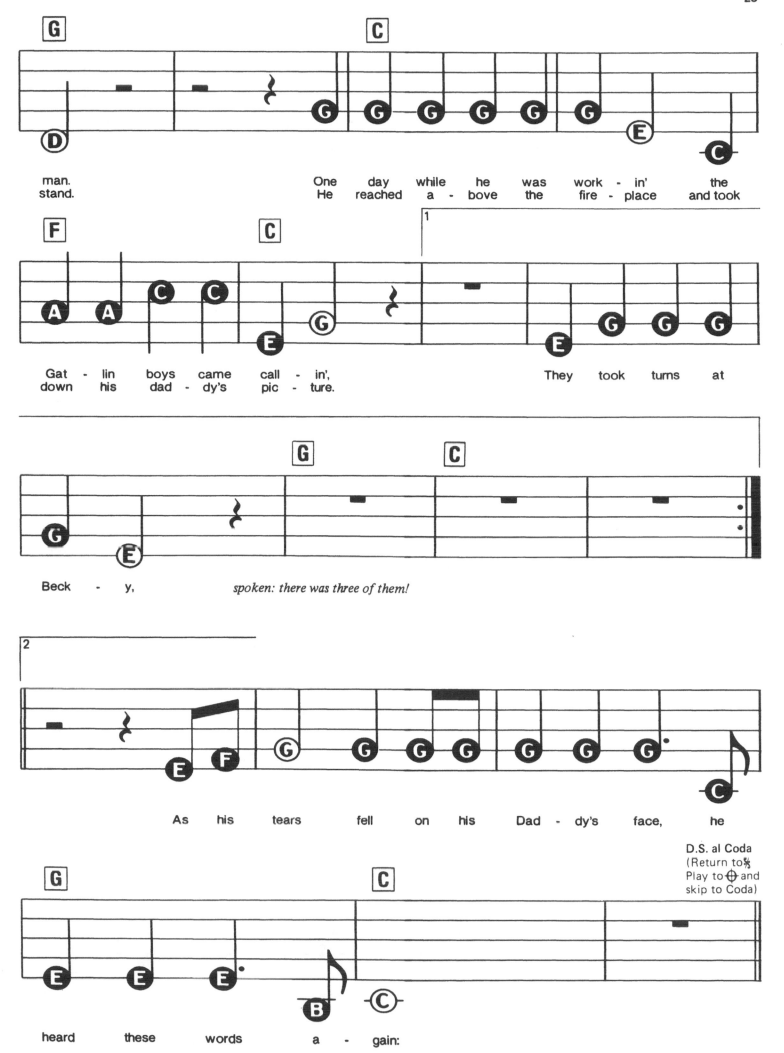

24

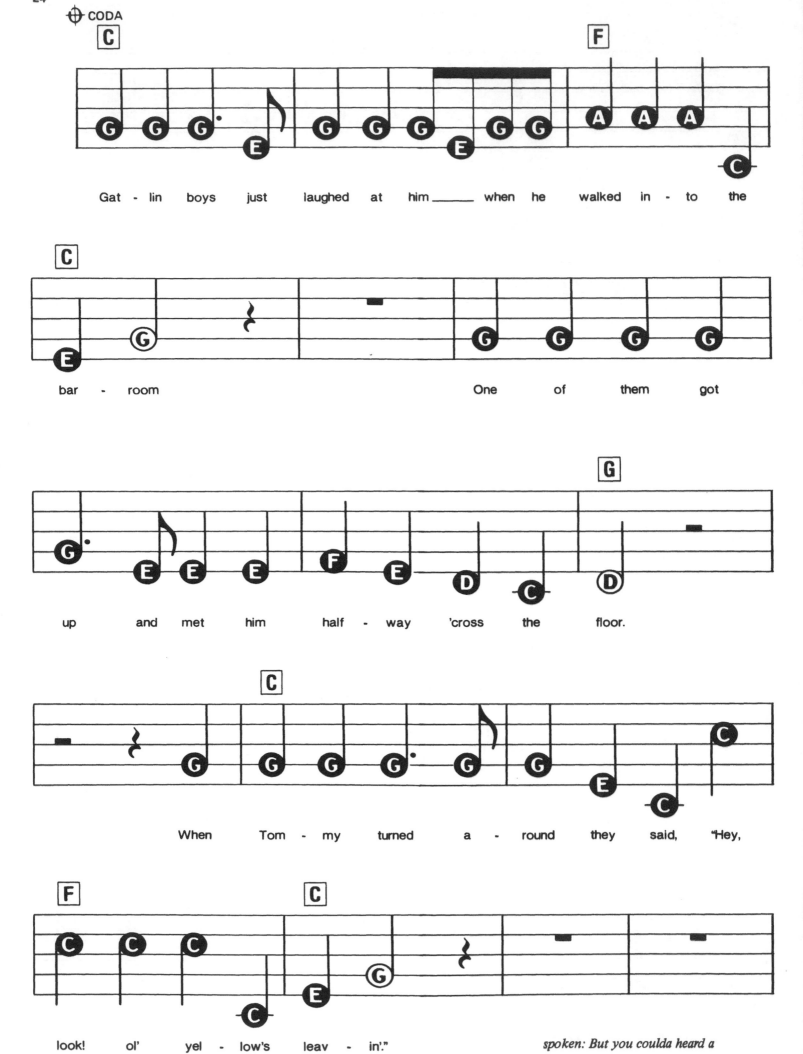

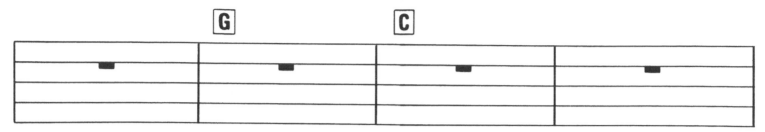

pin drop when Tommy stopped and blocked the door.

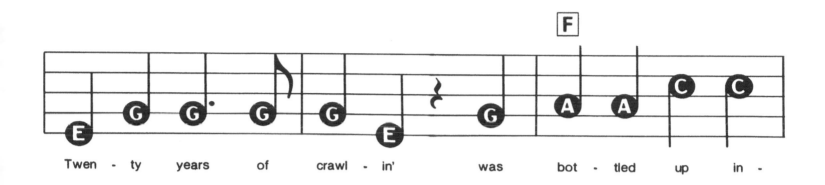

Twen - ty years of crawl - in' was bot - tled up in -

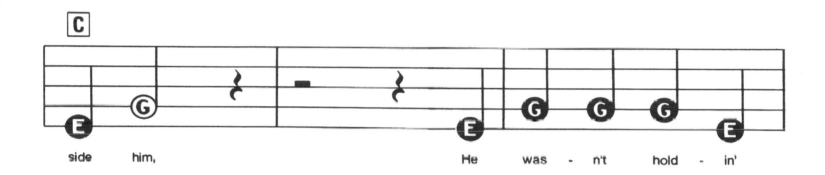

side him, He was - n't hold - in'

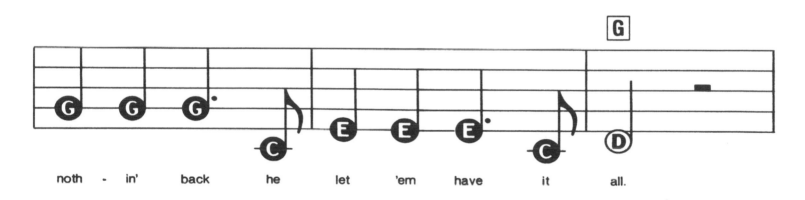

noth - in' back he let 'em have it all.

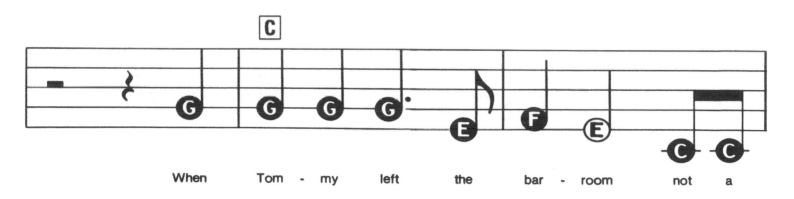

When Tom - my left the bar - room not a

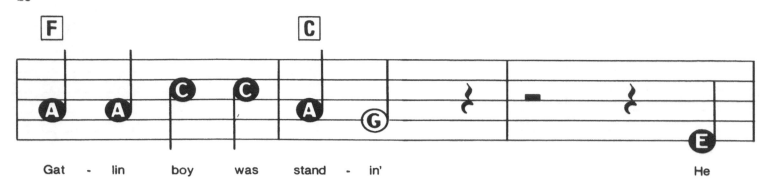

Gat - lin boy was stand - in' He

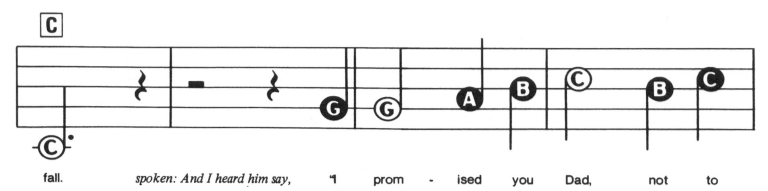

said, "This one's for Beck - y," As he watched the last one

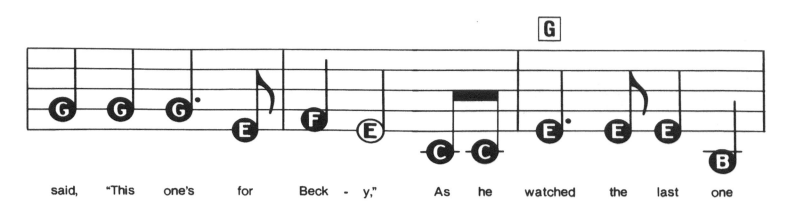

fall. *spoken: And I heard him say,* "I prom - ised you Dad, not to

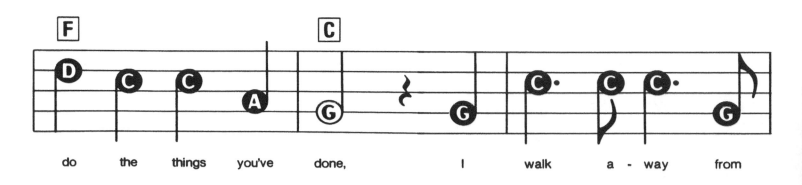

do the things you've done, I walk a - way from

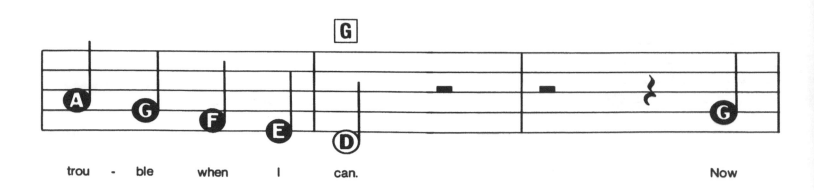

trou - ble when I can. Now

Every Time Two Fools Collide

Registration 3
Rhythm: Ballad

Words and Music by Jeff Tweel
and Jan Dyer

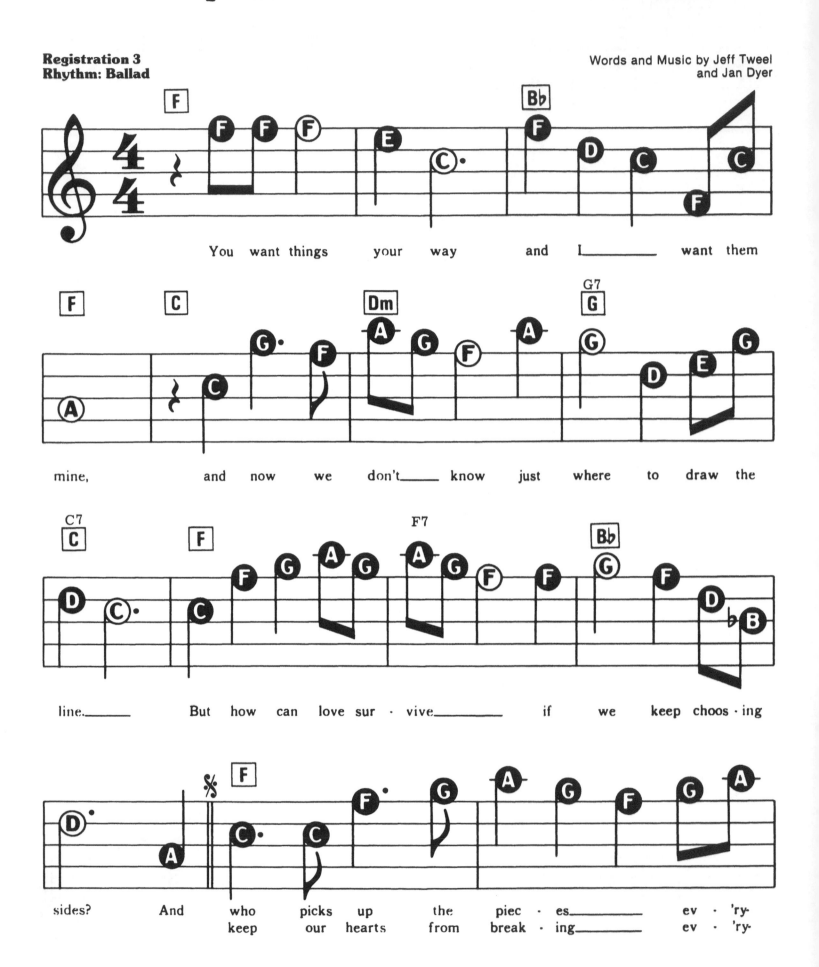

You want things your way and I_____ want them mine, and now we don't____ know just where to draw the line._____ But how can love sur · vive_____ if we keep choos · ing

sides? And
who picks up the piec · es_____ ev · 'ry-
keep our hearts from break · ing_____ ev · 'ry-

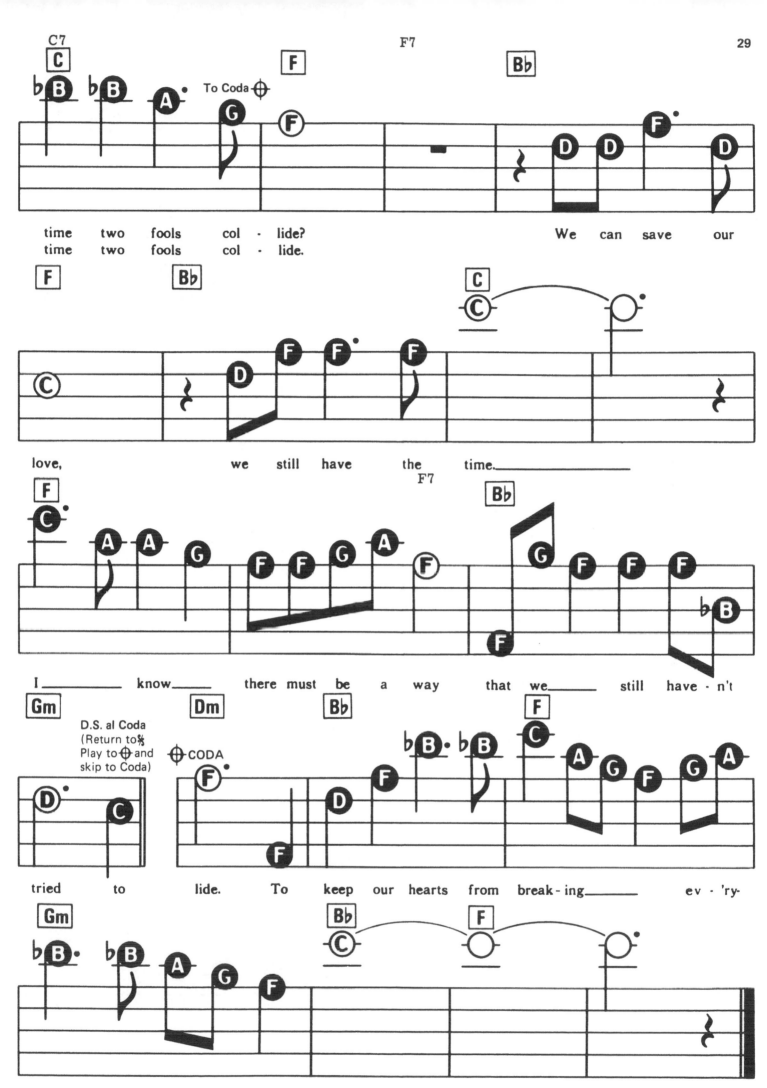

time   two   fools   col · lide?   We   can   save   our
time   two   fools   col · lide.

love,   we   still   have   the   time._____

I _____ know _____ there must be a way that we _____ still have·n't

tried   to   lide.   To   keep   our   hearts   from   break-ing _____   ev · 'ry-

time   two   fools _____   col · lide._____

Love Lifted Me

Registration 3
Rhythm: Country Waltz

Words and Music by Howard E. Smith,
James Rowe and Kenny Rogers

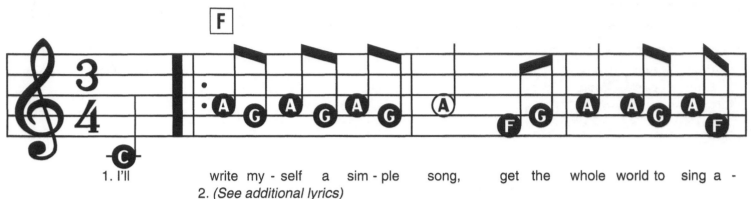

1. I'll write my - self a sim - ple song, get the whole world to sing a -
2. *(See additional lyrics)*

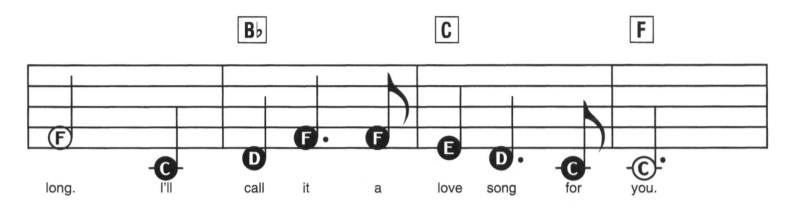

long. I'll call it a love song for you.

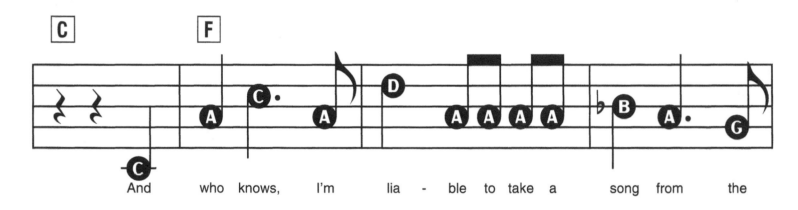

And who knows, I'm lia - ble to take a song from the

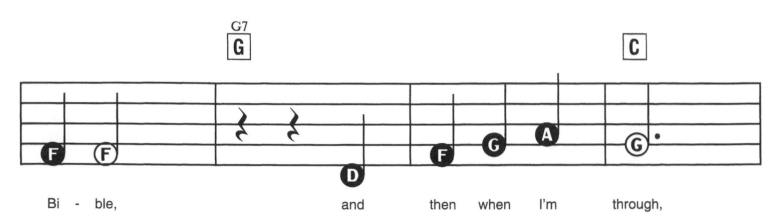

Bi - ble, and then when I'm through,

31

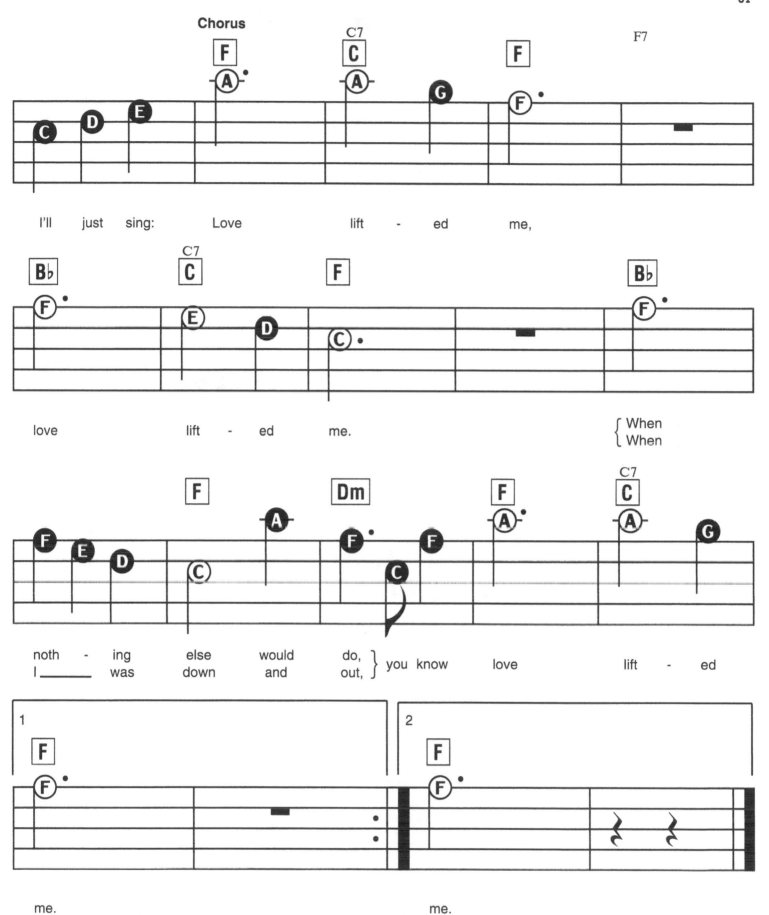

I'll just sing: Love lift - ed me,

love lift - ed me.

{ When
{ When

noth - ing else would do,
I _____ was down and out, } you know love lift - ed

1

me.

2

me.

Additional Lyrics

2. Everybody's lookin' for a way to say something.
   Everybody's sayin', "Well, that's hard to do."
   A-searchin' their mind, tryin' to find the one-of-a-kind way
   That they could say something new.
   I just say:
   Chorus

Morgana Jones

Registration 9
Rhythm: Country Western

Words and Music by Kenny Rogers

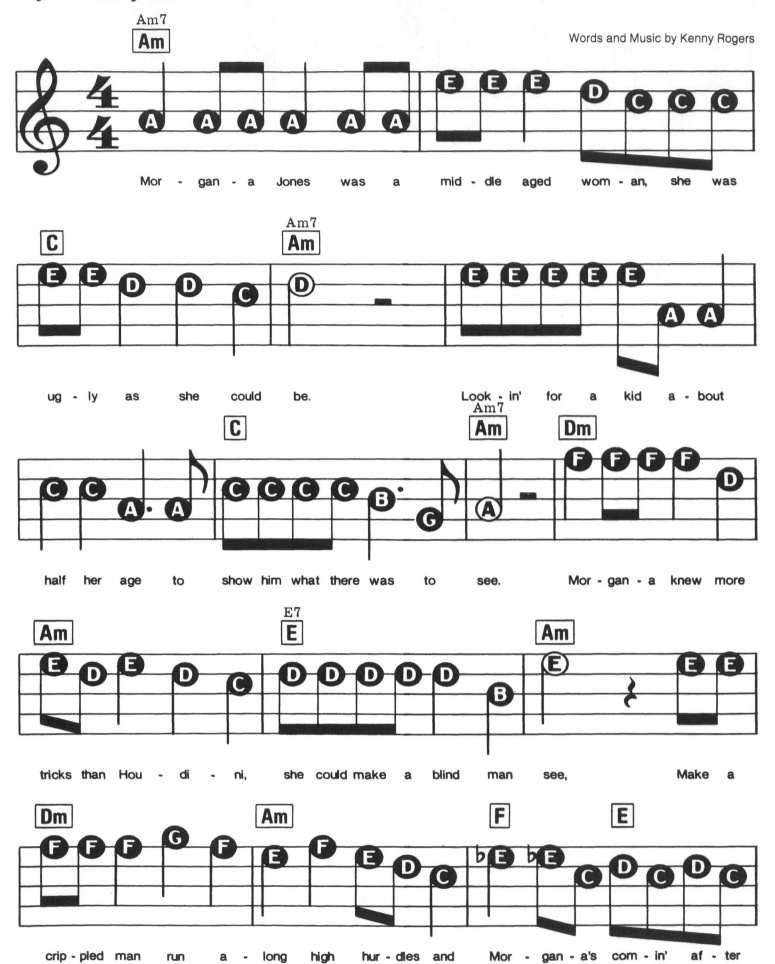

Mor - gan - a Jones was a mid - dle aged wom - an, she was

ug - ly as she could be. Look - in' for a kid a - bout

half her age to show him what there was to see. Mor - gan - a knew more

tricks than Hou - di - ni, she could make a blind man see, Make a

crip - pled man run a - long high hur - dles and Mor - gan - a's com - in' af - ter

33

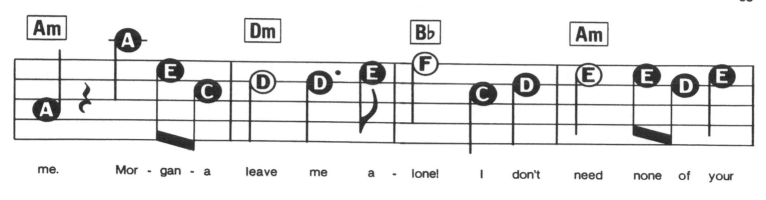

me. Mor - gan - a leave me a - lone! I don't need none of your

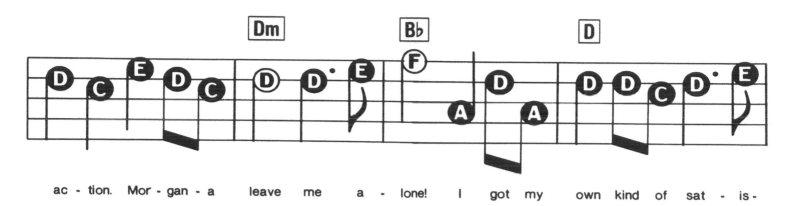

ac - tion. Mor - gan - a leave me a - lone! I got my own kind of sat - is -

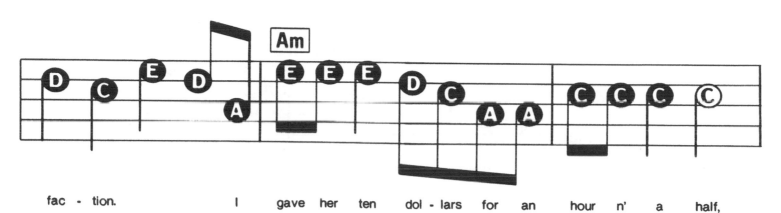

fac - tion. I gave her ten dol - lars for an hour n' a half,

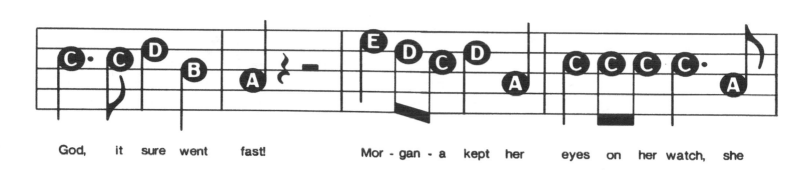

God, it sure went fast! Mor - gan - a kept her eyes on her watch, she

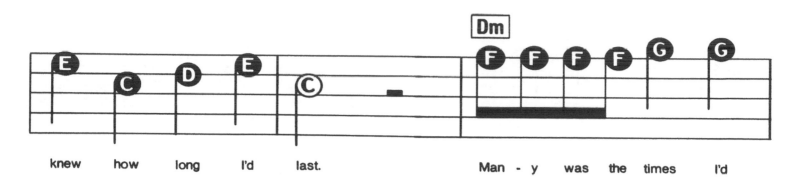

knew how long I'd last. Man - y was the times I'd

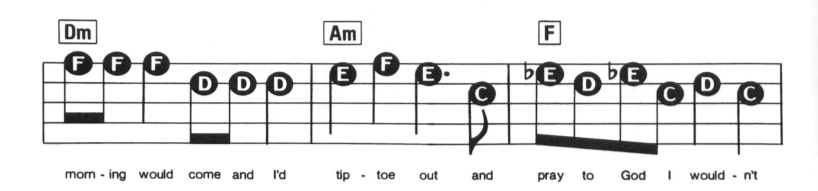

hide   up   in   the   hills,   it   was   that   or   the   un - der - tak - er.   And

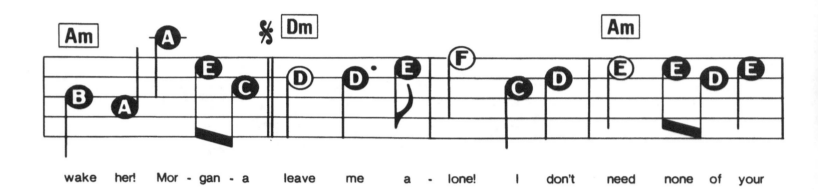

morn - ing   would   come   and   I'd   tip - toe   out   and   pray   to   God   I   would - n't

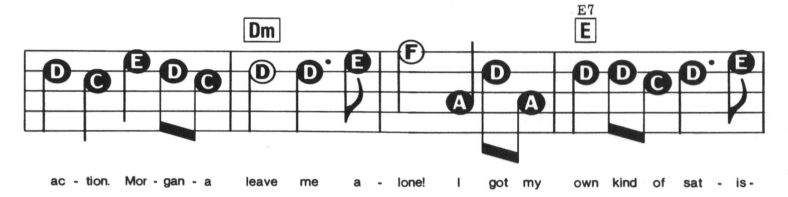

wake   her!   Mor - gan - a   leave   me   a - lone!   I   don't   need   none   of   your

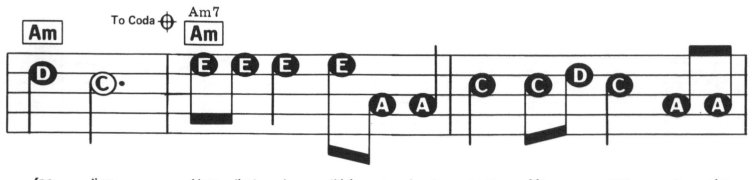

ac - tion.   Mor - gan - a   leave   me   a - lone!   I   got   my   own   kind   of   sat - is -

fac - tion.   Now   that   I   think   a - bout   poor   Mor - gan - a,   she

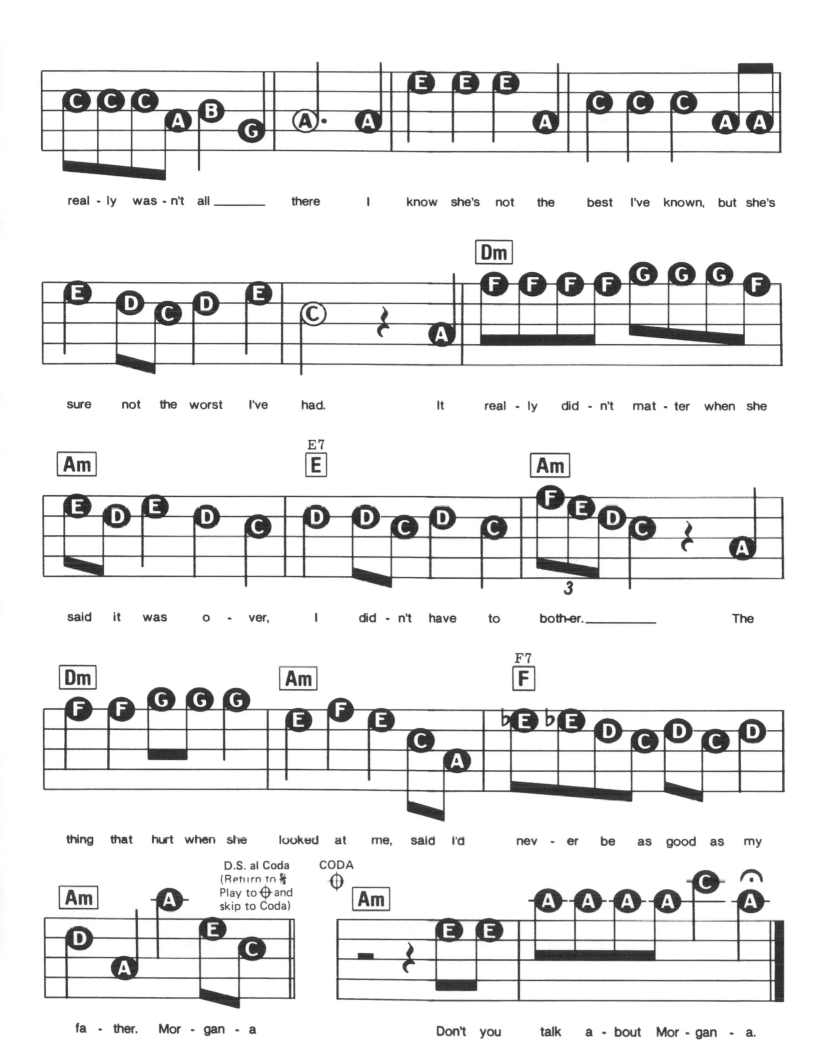

The Good Life

Registration 10
Rhythm: Waltz

Words and Music by Lionel Richie

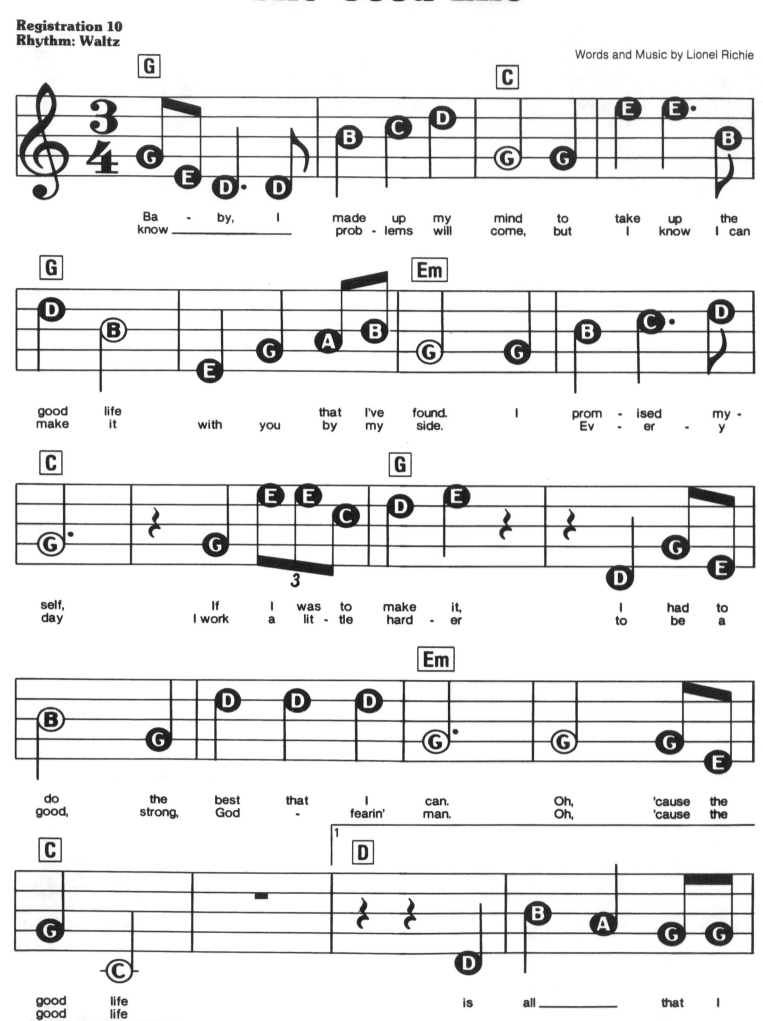

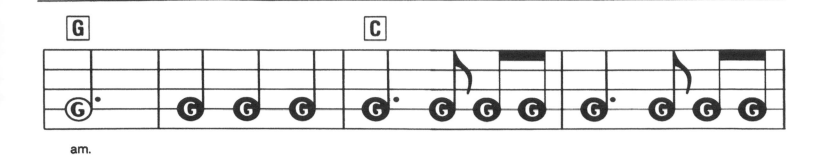

am.

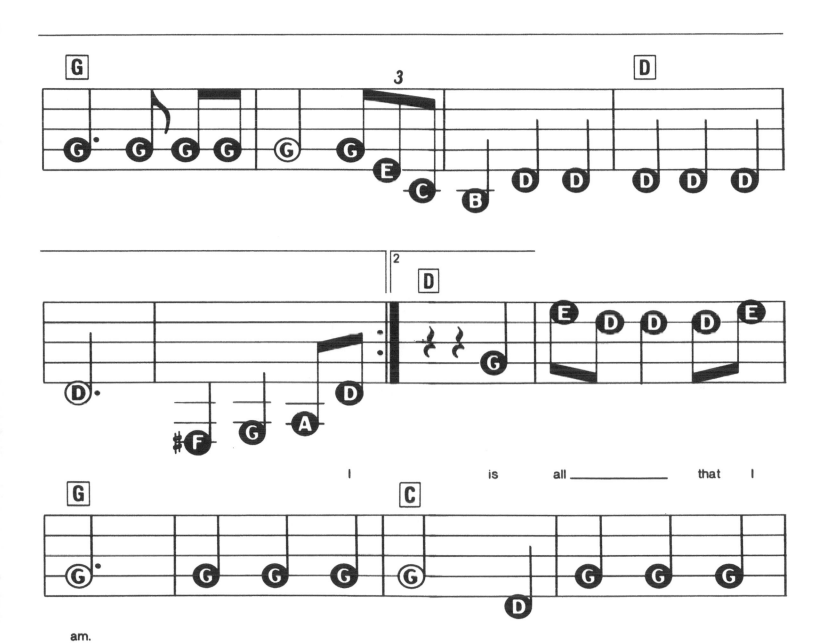

I   is   all _____ that   I

am.

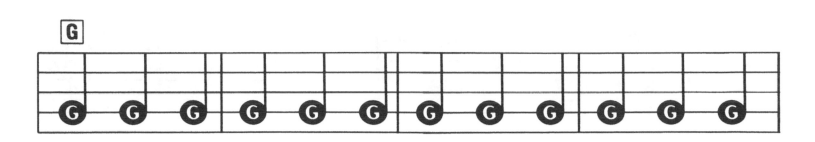

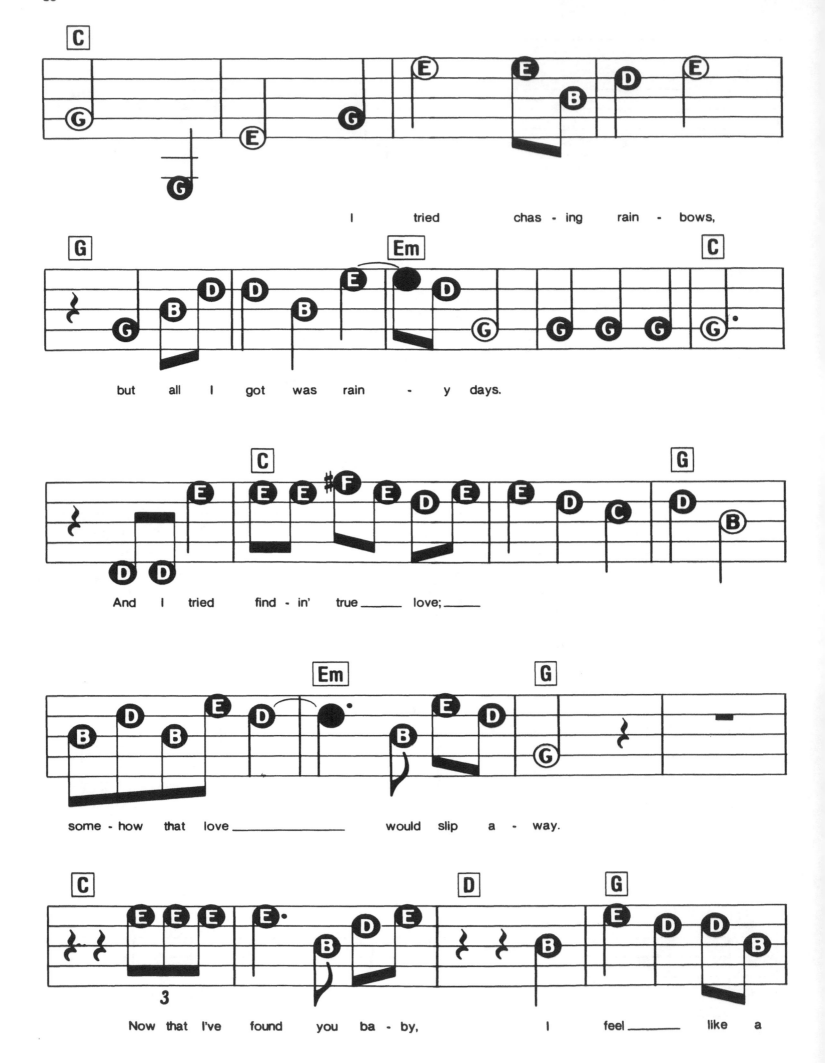

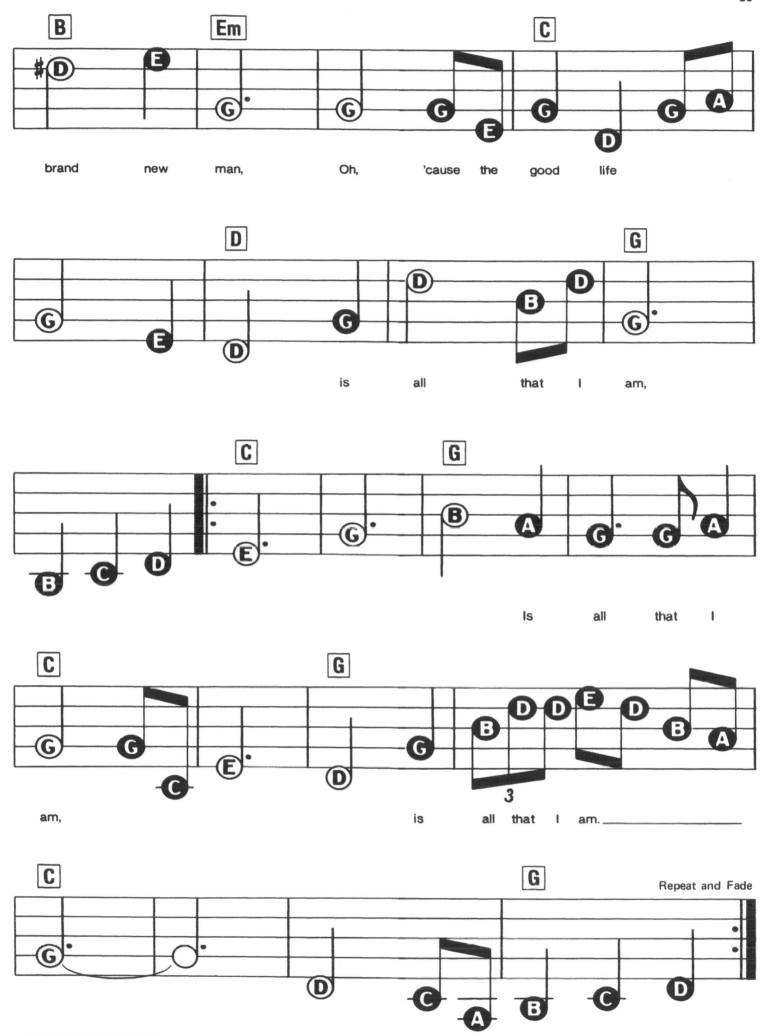

Long Arm Of The Law

Words and Music by
Roger Bowling and Billy Edd Wheeler

Registration 2
Rhythm: Country or Ballad

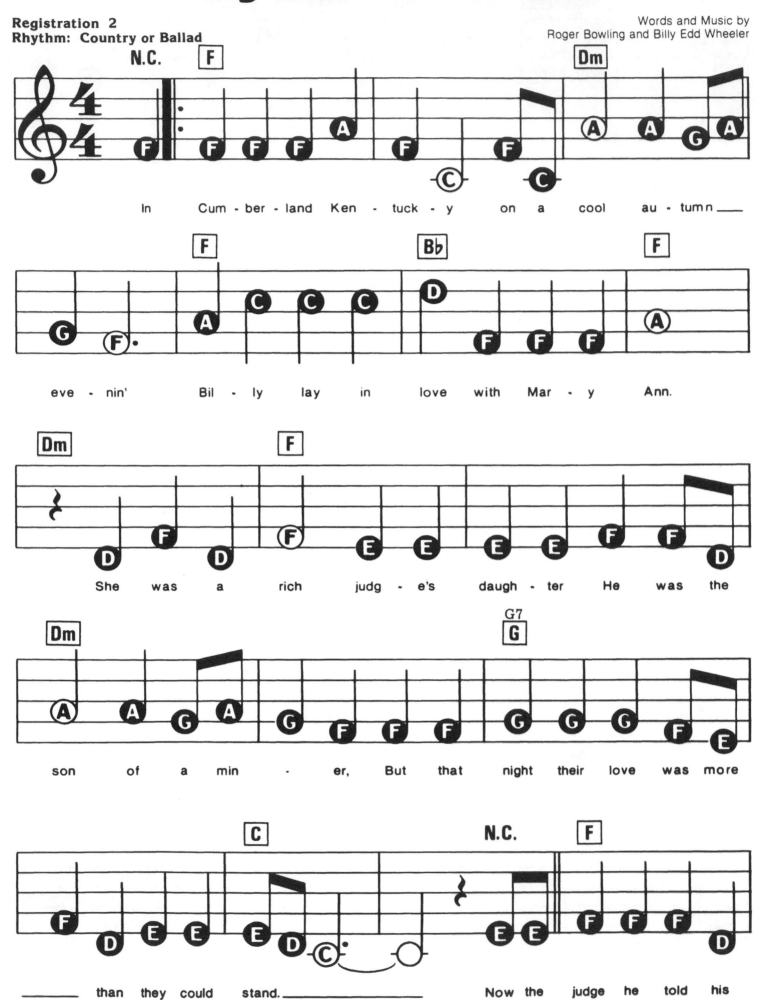

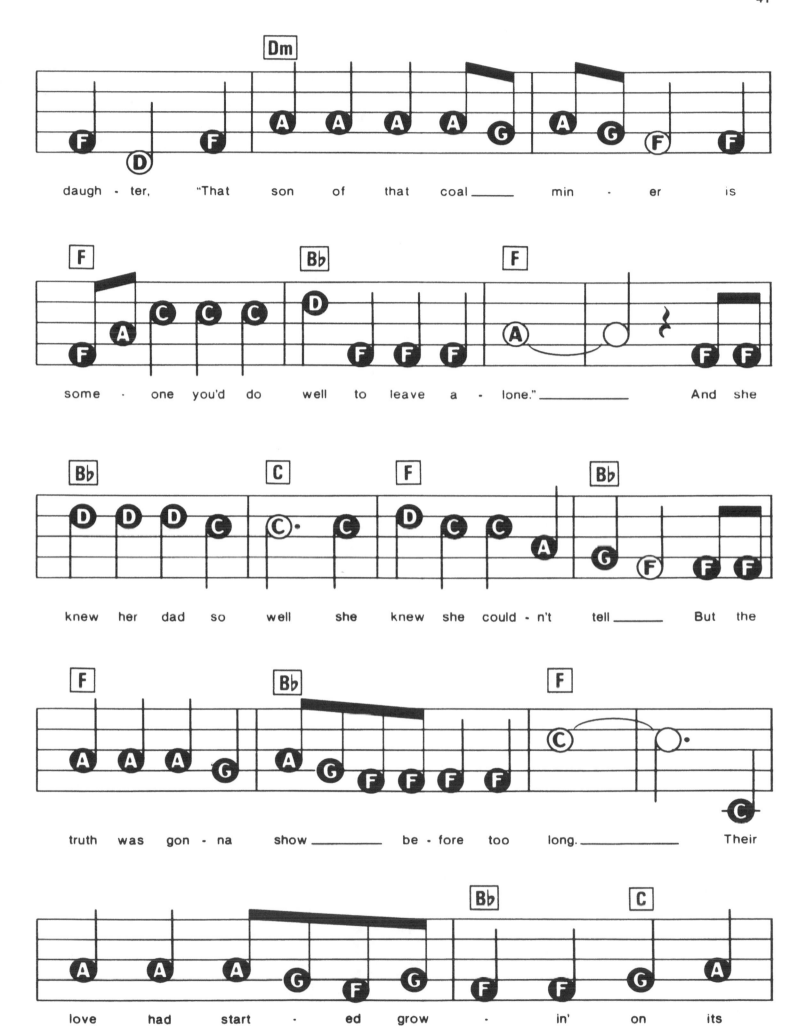

CHORUS

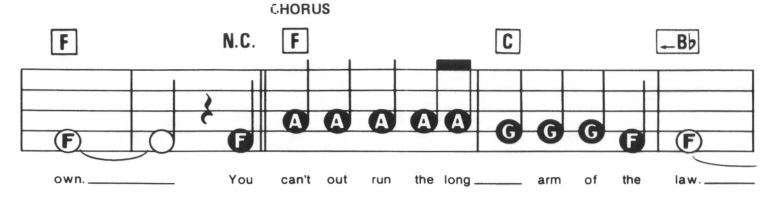

own. _____ You can't out run the long _____ arm of the law. _____

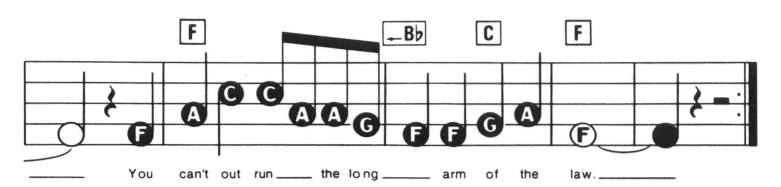

_____ You can't out run ____ the long _____ arm of the law. _____

Verse 2

Bill placed his hand on Mary and felt the baby movin'
Then he kissed her and said "I'll see you when I can,"
Cause the judge had made a promise when he caught up
    with Billy
He'd send him far away from Mary Ann.
The whole town knew he'd do it, too many times he'd
    proved it
To at least a hundred men behind, the walls
He'd smile beneath that frown and bring that gavel down
And call himself the long arm of the law
It seemed he liked to see a good man fall.
CHORUS:

Verse 3

In a hot, humid mineshaft, the mid-wife pulled the sheets back
And laid a cool, damp towel on Mary Ann
Billy's eyes were wide with wonder from the spell that he
    was under
When she placed the newborn baby in his hands
He didn't hear the siren, he only heard the baby cryin'
And that miracle of love is all he saw.
So when the door came crashin' down and Billy turned around,
He felt the heart and soul inside him fall
He stood face to face with the long arm of the law.
CHORUS:

Verse 4

They say everybody in Cumberland, Kentucky
Came down on that day to see the trial
When the court was called to order, there sat
    the judge's daughter
She looked so proud holdin' Billy's child.
When they brought Billy to him, that old
    judge looked right thru him
As he held that Holy Bible in his hand
He looked over at his grandson, then smiled back
    down at Billy
He said, "I think this time the law will understand.
Son, I sentence you to life . . . with Mary Ann.
CHORUS:

Love The World Away

Registration 2
Rhythm: Ballad

Words and Music by Bob Morrison
and Johnny Wilson

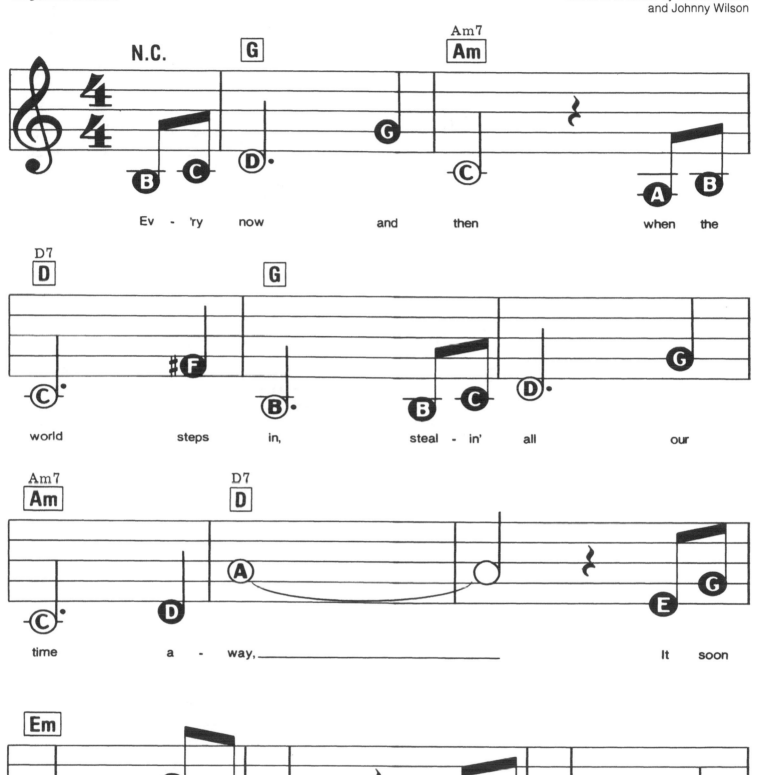

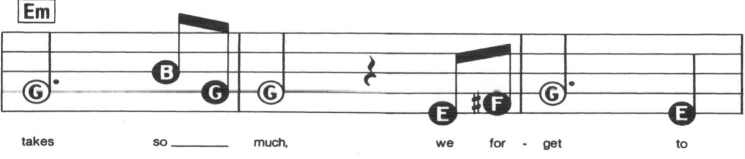

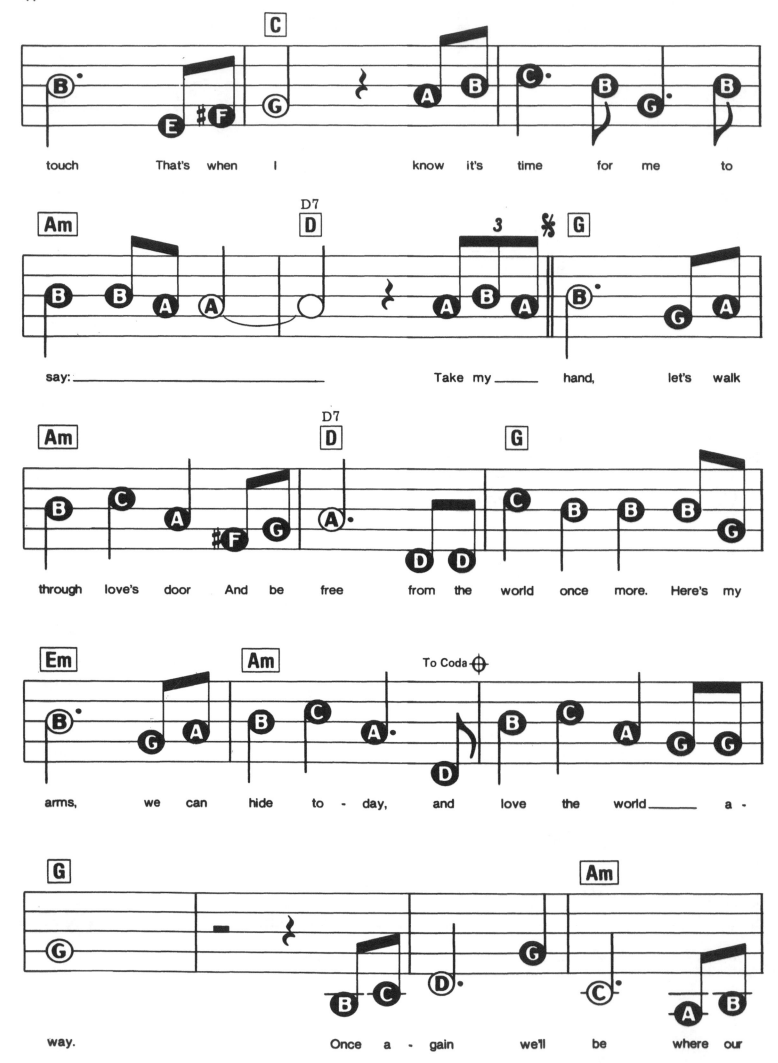

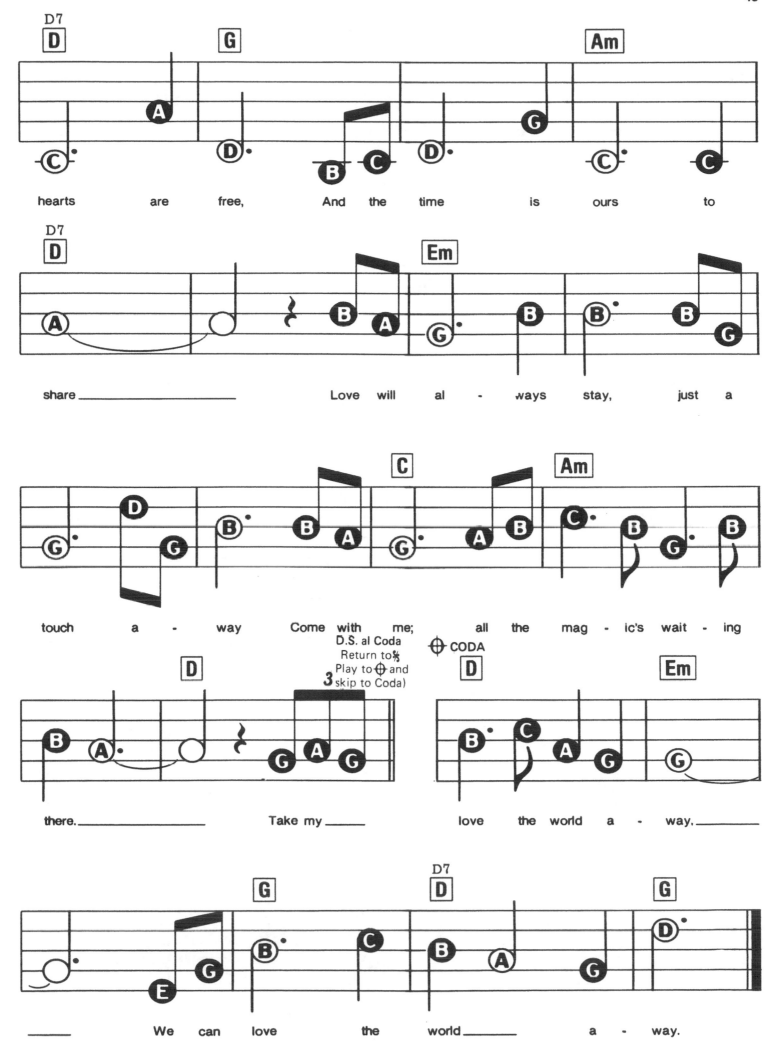

Lady

Words and Music by Lionel Richie, Jr.

Registration 3
Rhythm: Ballad

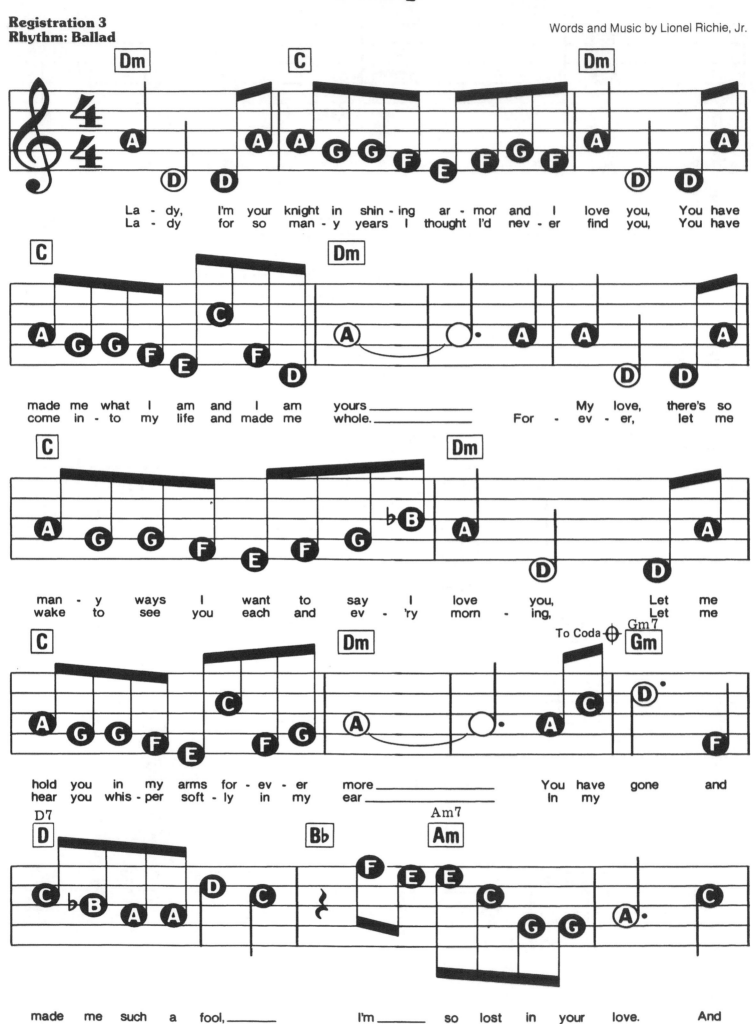

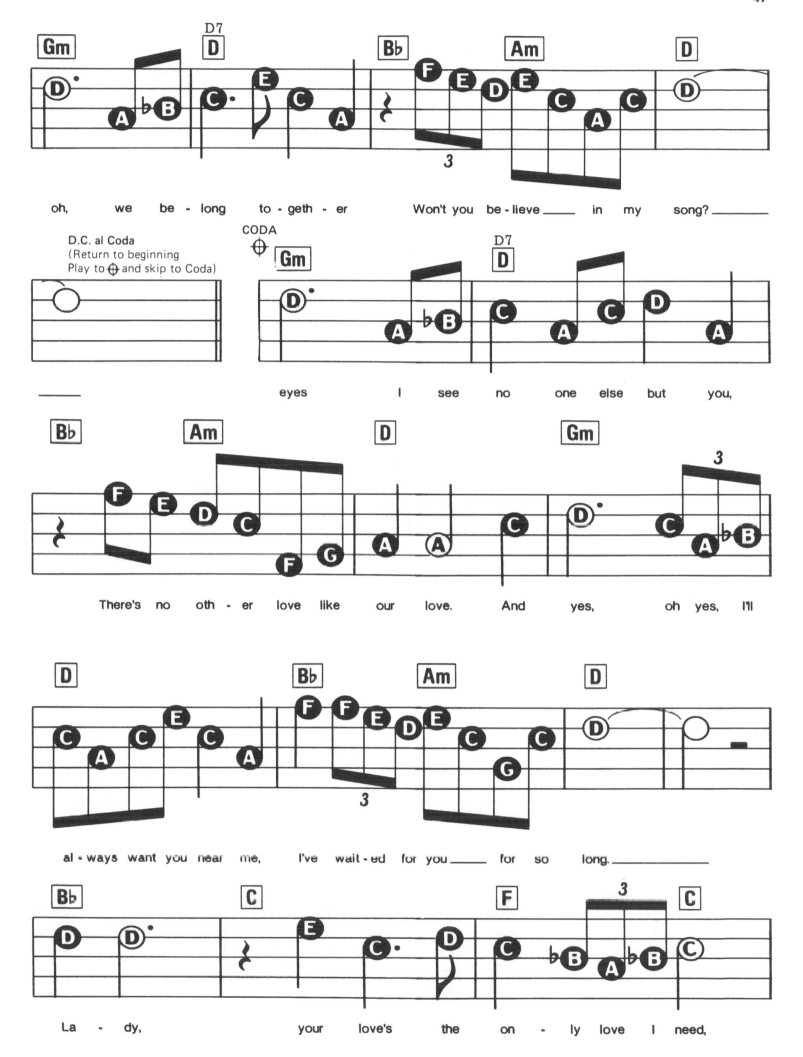

48

ALL I EVER NEED IS YOU

Words and Music by Jimmy Holiday and Eddie Reeves

Sometimes when I'm down and all alone
Just like a child without a home
The love you give me keeps me hangin' on
Oh honey, All I ever need is you

You're my first love, you're my last
You're my future, you're my past
And loving you is all I ask
Honey, all I ever need is you

Winters come and they go
And we watch the melting snow
Sure as summer follows spring
All the things you do give me a reason
To build my world around you

Some men follow rainbows, I am told
Some men search for silver some for gold
I have found my treasure in your soul
Honey, all I ever need is you

Without love I'd never find the way
Through ups and downs of ev'ry single day
I won't sleep at night until you say
My honey, all I ever need is you

COWARD OF THE COUNTY

Words and Music by Roger Bowling and Billy Edd Wheeler

Ev'ryone considered him
The coward of the county,
He'd never stood one single time
To prove the county wrong.
His mama named him Tommy
The folks just called him yellow,
But something always told me
They were readin' Tommy wrong.

He was only ten years old
When his daddy died in prison,
I looked after Tommy
'Cause he was my brother's son.
I still re-call the final words
My brother said to Tommy,
"Son, my life is over,
But yours is just begun.

Promise me, son,
Not to do the things I've done,
Walk away from trouble if you can.
It won't mean you're weak
If you turn the other cheek,
I hope you're old enough to understand:
Son, you don't have to fight to be a man."

There's someone for ev'ryone
And Tommy's love was Becky,
In her arms
He didn't have to prove he was a man.
One day while he was workin'
The Gatlin boys came callin',
They took turns at Becky,
There was three of them!

Tommy opened up the door
And saw his Becky cryin'
The torn dress the shattered look
Was more than he could stand.
He reached above the fireplace
And took down his daddy's picture,
As his tears fell on his Daddy's face,
He heard these words again:

Promise me, son,
Not to do the things I've done.
Walk away from trouble if you can.
It won't mean you're weak
If you turn the other cheek,
I hope you're old enough to understand:
Son, you don't have to fight to be a man.

The Gatlin boys just laughed at him
When he walked into the barroom
One of them got up
And met him half-way 'cross the floor.
When Tommy turned around they said,
"Hey look! ol' yellow's leavin'."
But you coulda heard a pin drop
When Tommy stopped and blocked the door.

Twenty years of crawlin'
Was bottled up inside him,
He wasn't holdin' nothin' back
He let 'em have it all.
When Tommy left the barroom
Not a Gatlin boy was standin'
He said, "This one's for Becky,"
As he watched the last one fall.

And I heard him say,
"I promise you Dad,
Not to do the things you've done,
I walk away from trouble when I can.
Now please don't think I'm weak,
I didn't turn the other cheek,
And Poppa I sure hope you understand:
Sometimes you gotta fight when you're a man."
Ev'ryone considered him
The coward of the county.

DAYTIME FRIENDS

Words and Music by Ben Peters

And he'll tell her he's working late again
But she knows too well there's something goin' on
She's been neglected and she needs a friend
So her trembling fingers dial the telephone

And Lord, it hurts her doin' this again
He's the best friend that her husband ever knew
When she's lonely, he's more than just a friend
He's the one she longs to give her body to

Daytime friends and nighttime lovers
Hoping no one else discovers
Where they go, what they do
In their secret hide-a-way

Daytime friends and nighttime lovers
They don't wanna hurt the others
So they love in the nighttime
And shake hands in the light of day

Daytime friends and nighttime lovers
Hoping no one else discovers
Where they go, what they do
In their secred hide-a-way

Daytime friends and nighttime lovers
They don't wanna hurt the others
So they love in the nighttime
And shake hands in the light of day

EVERY TIME TWO FOOLS COLLIDE

Words and Music by Jeff Tweel and Jan Dyer

You want things your way
And I want them mine
And now we don't know
Just where to draw the line

But how can love survive
If we keep choosing sides
And who picks up the pieces
Ev'rytime two fools collide

We can save our love
We still have the time
I know there must be a way
That we still haven't tried

To keep our hearts from breaking
Ev'rytime two fools collide
To keep our hearts from breaking
Ev'rytime two fools collide

THE GAMBLER

Words and Music by Don Schlitz

On a warm summer's evenin'
On a train bound for nowhere,
I met up with a gambler;
We were both too tired to sleep.
So we took turns a starin'
Out the window at the darkness
'Til boredom overtook us,
And he began to speak.

He said, "Son,
I've made a life out of readin' people's faces
And knowing what their cards were
By the way they held their eyes.
And if you don't mind my sayin',
I can see you're out of aces.
For a taste of your whiskey
I'll give you some advice."

So I handed him my bottle
And he drank down my last swallow.
Then he bummed a cigarette
And asked me for a light
And the night got deathly quiet,
And his face lost all expression.
Said, "If you're gonna play the game,
Boy, ya gotta learn to play it right.

You got to know when to hold 'em,
Know when to fold 'em,
Know when to walk away
And know when to run.
You never count your money
When you're sittin at the table,
There'll be time enough for countin'
When the dealin's done.

Ev'ry gambler knows
That the secret to survivin'
Is knowin' what to throw away,
And knowin' what to keep.
Cause ev'ry hand's a winner
And ev'ry hand's a loser,
And the best that you can hope for
Is to die in your sleep."

And when he'd finished speakin'
He turned back towards the window,
Crushed out his cigarette
And faded off to sleep.
And somewhere in the darkness
The gambler he broke even
But in his final words
I found an ace that I could keep.

You got to know when to hold 'em,
Know when to fold 'em,
Know when to walk away
And know when to run.
You never count your money
When you're sittin at the table,
There'll be time enough for countin'
When the dealin's done.

THE GOOD LIFE

Words and Music by Lionel Richie

Baby, I made up my mind
To take up the good life that I've found.
I promised myself, If I was to make it,
I had to do the best that I can.
Oh, 'cause the good life is all that I am.

I know problems will come,
But I know I can make it with you by my side.
Every day I work a little harder
To be a good, strong, God fearin' man.
Oh, 'cause the good life is all that I am.

I tried chasing rainbows,
But all I got was rainy days.
And I tried findin' true love;
Somehow that love would slip away.

Now that I've found you baby,
I feel like a brand new man,
Oh, 'cause the good life is all that I am,
Is all that I am, is all that I am.

LADY

Words and Music by Lionel Richie, Jr.

Lady, I'm your knight in shining armor
And I love you,
You have made me what I am
And I am yours.
My love, there's so many ways I want to say
I love you,
Let me hold you in my arms
Forever more.
You have gone and made me such a fool,
I'm so lost in your love.
And oh, we belong together
Won't you believe in my song?

Lady for so many years
I thought I'd never find you,
You have come into my life
And made me whole.
Forever, let me wake to see you
Each and ev'ry morning,
Let me hear you whisper
Softly in my ear
In my eyes I see no one else but you,
There's no other love like our love.

And yes, oh yes,
I'll always want you near me,
I've waited for you for so long.
Lady, your love's the only love I need,
And beside me
Is where I want you to be.
Cause my love,
There's something I want you to know.
You're the love of my life,
You're my lady.

LONG ARM OF THE LAW

Words and Music by Roger Bowling and Billy Edd Wheeler

In Cumberland, Kentucky on a cool autumn evenin'
Billy lay in love with Mary Ann
She was a rich judge's daughter
He was the son of a miner
But that night their love was more than they could stand
Now the judge he told his daughter
"That son of that coal miner
Is someone you'd do well to leave alone"
And she knew her dad so well
She knew she couldn't tell
But the truth was gonna show before too long
Their love had started growin' on its own
You can't out run the long arm of the law
You can't out run the long arm of the law

Bill placed his hand on Mary and felt the baby movin'
The he kissed her and said "I'll see you when I can"
Cause the judge had made a promise
When he caught up with Billy
He'd send him far away from Mary Ann
The whole town knew he'd do it
Too many times he'd proved it
To at least a hundred men behind the walls
He'd smile beneath that frown and bring that gavel down
And call himself the long arm of the law
It seemed he liked to see a good man fall

In a hot, humid mineshaft, the mid-wife pulled the sheets back
And laid a cool, damp towel on Mary Ann
Billy's eyes were wide with wonder
From the spell that he was under
When she placed the newborn baby in his hands
He didn't hear the siren, he only heard the baby cryin'
And that miracle of love is all he saw
So when the door came crashin' down and Billy turned around
He felt the heart and soul inside him fall
He stood face to face with the long arm of the law

They say everybody in Cumberland, Kentucky
Came down on that day to see the trial
When the court was called to order
There sat the judge's daughter
She looked so proud holdin' Billy's child
When they brought Billy to him
That old judge looked right thru him
As he held that Holy Bible in his hand
He looked over at his grandson
Then smiled back down at Billy
He said, "I think this time the law will understand
Son, I sentence you to life. . .with Mary Ann

54

LOVE LIFTED ME
Words and Music by Howard E. Smith,
James Rowe and Kenny Rogers

I'll write myself a simple song,
Get the whole world to sing along.
I'll call it a love song for you.
And who knows, I'm liable to take a song from the Bible,
And then when I'm through, I'll just sing:

Love lifted me,
Love lifted me.
When nothing else would do,
You know love lifted me.

Everybody's lookin' for a way to say something.
Everybody's sayin', "Well, that's hard to do."
A-searchin' their mind, tryin' to find the one-of-a-kind way
That they could say something new.
I just say:

Love lifted me,
Love lifted me.
When I was down and out,
You know love lifted me.

LOVE OR SOMETHING LIKE IT
Words and Music by Kenny Rogers and Steve Glassmeyer

Show me a bar with a good-looking woman,
Then just get out of my way.
Turn on the jukebox,
I'll show you a song you should play.
Sooner or later, a few shots of bourbon,
I'll think of something to say.
Wo, I can take her or leave her.
I'd like to take her away.

Liquor and music a good combination
If you've got love on the brain.
I never knew two women
Who acted the same:
Some want a drink first
And some want to just sit and talk.
Wo, it's two in the morning.
I'm running and she wants to walk.

Something's got a hold on me,
It's cheap but it ain't free.
Love or something like it's got a hold on me.

That's when I asked her,
"My place or your place?
I hope I'm not out of line."
I asked the wrong thing to just the right woman this time.
She knew a hotel,
She even had a name we could sign.
Wo, the cheaper the grapes are,
The sweeter the taste of the wine.

Something's got a hold on me,
It's cheap but it ain't free.
Love or something like it's got a hold on me.
Love or something damn near like it's got a hold on me.

A LOVE SONG

Words and Music by Lee Greenwood

Why do people cry when they hear the word goodbye
In a love song?
Tears are sure to fall when you know they gave it all
In a love song.
Somehow two lovers got a chance at a beautiful romance
And you wish it could be you,
'Cause everybody's needin' what the singers all are singin'
In a love song.

It can tear you apart 'cause a word can break your heart
In a love song.
They say all the things you feel, and they make it sound so real
In a love song.
It seems that everything they say is said in such a way
That we believe it's true.
'Cause everybody's needin' what the singers all are singin'
In a love song.

Each of us know there's no guarantee we'll ever find love,
And in the songs that we share the heartache is there
To remind us.
New love brings a thrill and we know it always will
In a love song.
Happiness can leave but it helps if we believe
In a love song.

There's a part of you and me in ev'ry memory
That tells us who we are.
And everybody's needin' what the singers are all singin'
In a love song.
And everybody's needin' what the singers are all singin'
In a love song.

LOVE THE WORLD AWAY

Words and Music by Bob Morrison and Johnny Wilson

Ev'ry now and then when the world steps in,
Stealin' all our time away,
It soon takes so much, we forget to touch
That's when I know it's time for me to say:

Take my hand, let's walk through loves door
And be free from the world once more.
Here's my arms, we can hide today,
And love the world away.

Once again we'll be where our hearts are free,
And the time is ours to share
Love will always stay, just a touch away
Come with me; all the magic's waiting there.

Take my hand, let's walk through loves door
And be free from the world once more.
Here's my arms, we can hide today,
And love the world away.
We can love the world away.

LUCILLE

Words and Music by Roger Bowling and Hal Bynum

In a bar in Toledo
Across from the depot
On a bar stool she took off her ring
I thought I'd get closer
So I walked on over
I sat down and asked her her name

When the drinks fin'lly hit her
She said: I'm no quitter
But I fin'lly quit living on dreams
I'm hungry for laughter and here ever after
I'm after whatever the other life brings

In the mirror I saw him
And I closely watched him
I thought how he looked out of place
He came to the woman
Who sat there beside me
He had a strange look on his face

The big hands were calloused
He looked like a mountain
For a minute I thought I was dead
But he started shaking
His big heart was breaking
And turned to the woman and said

You picked a fine time to leave me, Lucille
With four hungry children and a crop in the field
I've had some bad times
Lived through some sad times
But this time your hurtin' won't heal
You picked a fine time to leave me, Lucille

MAKING MUSIC FOR MONEY

Words and Music by Alex Harvey

I woke up this mornin',
I was tired as I could be;
I guess I was countin' my money
When I should have been countin' sheep.
My agent he just called me,
And he told me what I should be.
He said that I should make my music for money
Instead of makin' my music for me.
And I said, "I know that it may sound funny,
But money don't mean nothin' to me.
I won't make my music for money,
I'm gonna make my music for me."

Now people only like a love song,
Rock-an-roll an' not too long.
He say, "Kid you got to be commercial
If you wanta turn the people on."
Now turnin' on the people
What a beautiful place to be,
But if I spend my time makin' them up a rhyme,
Who's gonna turn on me? And I said,
"I know that it may sound funny
But money don't mean nothin' to me.
I won't make my music for money,
I'm gonna make my music for me."

I went up the country
And I'll tell you about the scene:
I found a place with much charm and much grace
That wasn't touched by the music machine.
The people were havin' a good time,
Ev'rybody singin' a-long.
And nobody cared if nobody gave them
A penny for singin' a song.
And I said, "I know that it may sound funny
But money don't mean nothin' to me.
I won't make my music for money,
I'm gonna make my music for me."

I said, "I know that it may sound funny
But money don't mean nothin' to me.
I won't make my music for money
I'm gonna make my music for,
Make my music for, make my music for me."

MORGANA JONES

Words and Music by Kenny Rogers

Morgana Jones was a middle aged woman,
She was ugly as she could be.
Lookin' for a kid about half her age
To show him what there was to see
Morgana knew more tricks than Houdini,
She could make a blind man see.
Make a crippled man run along high hurdles
And Morgana's comin' after me.

Morgana leave me alone!
I don't need none of your action.
Morgana leave me alone!
I got my own kind of satisfaction.
I gave her ten dollars for a hour n' a half,
God, it sure went fast!
Morgana kept her eyes on her watch,
She knew how long I'd last.

Many was the times I'd hide up in the hills,
It was that or the undertaker.
And morning would come and I'd tip-toe out
And pray to God I wouldn't hate her!
Morgana leave me alone!
I don't need none of your action.
Morgana leave me alone!
I got my own kind of satisfaction.

Now that I think about poor Morgana,
She really wasn't all there
I know she's not the best I've known,
But she's sure not the worst I've had.
It really didn't matter when she said it was over,
I didn't have to bother.
The thing that hurt when she looked at me,
Said I'd never be as good as my father.

Morgana leave me alone!
I don't need none of your action.
Morgana leave me alone!
I got my own kind of satisfaction.
Don't you talk about Morgana.

REUBEN JAMES

Words and Music by Alex Harvey and Barry Etris

Reuben James,
In my song you'll live again.
And the phases that I rhyme
As just the foot-steps out of time.
From the time when I knew you,
Reuben James

Reuben James,
All the Folks around Madison County cussed your name.
You're just a no-account share croppin' colored man
Who would steal anything he can,
And ev'rybody laid the blame on Reuben James.

Reuben James,
You still walk the furthest fields of my mind.
Faded shirt, the weathered brow,
The calloused hands upon the plow,
I loved you then and I love you now
Reuben James.

Flora Gray,
The gossip of Madison County died with Child.
And although your skin was black,
You were the one that didn't turn your back
On the hungry white child with no name,
Reuben James.

Reuben James,
With your mind on the soul and a bottle in your right hand.
You said, "Turn the other cheek
'Cause there's a better world awaitin' for the meek."
In my mind these words remain from a Reuben James.

Reuben James,
You still walk the furthest fields of my mind.
Faded shirt, the weathered brow,
The calloused hands upon the plow,
I loved you then and I love you now
Reuben James.

Reuben James,
One dark cloudy day they brought you from the field.
Until your lonely pine box came,
A just a picture me in the rain
Just to sing one last refrain for Reuben James.

Reuben James,
You still walk the furthest fields of my mind.
Faded shirt, the weathered brow,
The calloused hands upon the plow,
I loved you then and I love you now Reuben James.
Reuben James.

RUBY, DON'T TAKE YOUR LOVE TO TOWN
Words and Music by Mel Tillis

You've painted up your lips
And rolled and curled your tinted hair;
Ruby, are you contemplating going out somewhere?
The shadow on the wall
Tells me the sun is goin' down.
Oh, Ruby, don't take your love to town.

It wasn't me that started that old crazy Asian war,
But I was proud to go and do my patriotic chore.
And yes it's true that I'm not the man I used to be,
Oh, Ruby, I still need some company.

It's hard to love a man
Whose legs are bent and paralyzed,
And the wants and the needs of a woman your age,
Ruby, I realize.
But it won't be long I've heard them say
Until I'm not around,
Oh Ruby, Don't take your love to town.

She's leavin' now
'Cause I just heard the slammin' of the door,
The way I know I've heard it slam
One hundred times before,
And if I could move
I'd get my gun and put her in the ground,
Oh, Ruby, Don't take your love to town.
Oh, Ruby, For God's sake, turn around!

SHE BELIEVES IN ME
Words and Music by Steve Gibb

While she lays sleeping
I stay out late at night and play my songs
And sometimes all the nights can be so long
And it's good when I fin'ly make it home
All alone

While she lays dreaming
I try to get undressed without the light
Then quietly she says, "How was your night?"
And I come to her and say it was all right
And I hold her tight

And she believes in me
I'll never know just what she sees in me
I told her someday if she was my girl
I could change the world with my little songs
I was wrong

But she has faith in me
And so I go on trying faithfully
And who knows maybe on some special night
If my song is right
I will find a way, find a way

While she lays waiting
I stumble to the kitchen for a bite
Then I see my old guitar in the night
Just waiting for me like a secret friend
And there's no end

While she lays crying
I fumble with a melody or two
Then I'm torn between the things that I should do
Then she says to wake her up when I am through
God, her love is true

And she believes in me
I'll never know just what she sees in me
I told her someday if she was my girl
I could change the world with my little songs

I was wrong
But she has faith in me
And so I go on trying faithfully
And who knows maybe on some special night
If my song is right
I will find a way while she waits for me.

SO IN LOVE WITH YOU
Words and Music by Lionel Richie

Girl, I'll sing you love songs ev'ry mornin',
By my side you'll never be alone.
Just tell me what it is your heart desires,
'Cause all I want to do is take you home.

Cause I'm so in love with you,
Yes, I'm so in love with you,
Yes, I'm so in love with you,
I'm so in love with you.

Come on girl, I need you here beside me,
I'll show you love like you've never known.
And I won't tell the world how much I love you,
'Cause all I want to do is take you home.

'Cause I'm so in love with you,
Yes, I'm so in love with you,
Yes, I'm so in love with you,
I'm so in love with you.

Say "yes", it only takes a minute.
Your love I've got to win it; Don't let me down.
You know there's one thing about 'cha.
I just can't live without 'cha, Don't let me down Yeah

You're the one that keeps me all together,
Let me hold you in my arms all through the night.
What I'm tryin' to say is "Girl, I love you,
And lovin' you's the best part of my life."

'Cause I'm so in love with you,
Yes, I'm so in love with you,
Yes, I'm so in love with you,
I'm so in love with you.

Oh, yeah. So in love with you,
I can't help myself, baby.
So in love with you, girl.

SWEET MUSIC MAN
Words and Music by Kenny Rogers

I wouldn't listen, and I couldn't see,
And all I have left now are words you said to me.
Sing your song, sweet music man,
'Cause I won't be there to hold your hand like I used to;
I'm through with you.

You're a hell of a singer and a powerful man,
But you surround yourself with people who demand so little of you.
You touched my soul with your beautiful song,
You even had me singin' along right with you;
You said I need you.

Then you changed the words and added harmony,
And you sang the song you had written for me to someone new.
But nobody sings a love song quite like you do,
And nobody else could make me sing along,
And nobody else could make me feel
That things are right when I know they're wrong.
Nobody sings a love song quite like you.

Sing your song, sweet music man,
You travel the world with a six piece band
That does for you what you ask 'em to.
And you try to stay young but the songs
You've sung to so many people;

They've all begun to come back on you.
So sing your song, sad music man,
You're makin' your livin' doin' one-night stands
That proves to you they don't need you.
You're still a hell of a singer but a broken man,
But you'll keep on lookin' for one last fan to sing 'em to.

But nobody sings a love song quite like you do,
And nobody else could make me sing along,
And nobody else could make me feel
That things are right when I know they're wrong.
Nobody sings a love song quite like you.
Sing your song, sweet music man,
I believe in you.

THERE'S AN OLD MAN IN OUR TOWN

Words and Music by Kenny Rogers

There's an old man in our town,
And I guess he's been around for years and years,
At least it seems that way.
Wrinkled hands and rocking chair,
Growing old just sitting there;
Ev'ry year he has the same old thing to say.

Youth only happens to you one time.
And so I've been told.
If you should miss it in your young time.
Have it when you're old.

Now there's no old man sitting there,
Just an empty rocking chair.
But the things he said will always be around.
Some day when I'm old and gray,
Maybe youth can come my way.
I'll be proud to be the old man in our town.

And I say Youth only happens to you one time.
And so I've been told.
If you should miss it in your young time.
Have it when you're old.

THROUGH THE YEARS

Words and Music by Steve Dorff and Marty Panzer

I can't remember when you weren't there
When I didn't care for anyone but you
I swear we've been through everything there is
Can't imagine anything we've missed
Can't imagine anything the two of us can't do

Through the years you've never let me down
You've turned my life around
The sweetest days I've found
I've found with you through the years

I've never been afraid
I've loved the life we've made
And I'm so glad I've stayed
Right here with you through the years

I can't remember what I used to do
Who I trusted who I listened to before
I swear you've taught me everything I know
Can't imagine needing someone so

But through the years it seems to me
I need you more and more
Through the years through all the good and bad
I knew how much we had
I've always been so glad to be with you

Through the years it's better every day
You've kissed my tears away
As long as it's okay
I'll stay with you through the years

Through the years when everything went wrong
Together we were strong
I know that I belonged right here with you

Through the years I never had a doubt
We'd always work things out
I've learned what love's about
By loving you through the years

Through the years you've never let me down
You turned my life around
The sweetest days I've found I've found with you

Through the years it's better every day
You've kissed my tears away
As long as it's okay
I'll stay with you through the years

WITHOUT YOU IN MY LIFE

Words and Music by Lionel Richie and Thomas McClary

Life's winding roads may be lonely,
And we may never pass this way again; So let's be friends.
I know our problems come between us,
But there's one thing you must understand:
I wanna be your man.
'Cause girl, I'm never gonna find that love,
I'm never gonna find that dream without you in my life.

I love those times we were together,
You know I'll always need you by my side to be my guide.
Now all our cards are on the table,
I sure hope we played our aces well, but time will tell.

'Cause girl, I'm never gonna find that love,
I'm never gonna find that dream without you in my life.
'Cause girl, I'm never gonna find that love.
I'm never gonna find that dream without you in my life,
Oh girl, I'm never gonna find that love,
I'm never gonna find that dream without you in my life,
In my life, in my life, in my life. . .

YOU DECORATED MY LIFE

Words and Music by Bob Morrison and Debbie Hupp

All my life was a paper
Once plain, pure and white
Till you moved with your pen
Changin' moods now and then
Till the balance was right

Then you added some music
Ev'ry note was in place
And anybody could see
All the changes in me
By the look on my face

And you decorated my life
Created a world where dreams are apart
And you decorated my life
By paintin' your love all over my heart
You decorated my life

Like a rhyme with no reason
In an unfinished song
There was no harmony
Life meant nothin' to me
Until you came along

And you brought out the colors
What a gentle surprise
Now I'm able to see
All the things life can be
Shinin' soft in your eyes

And you decorated my life
Created a world where dreams are apart
And you decorated my life
By paintin' your love all over my heart
You decorated my life

She Believes In Me

Registration 5
Rhythm: Ballad

Words and Music by Steve Gibb

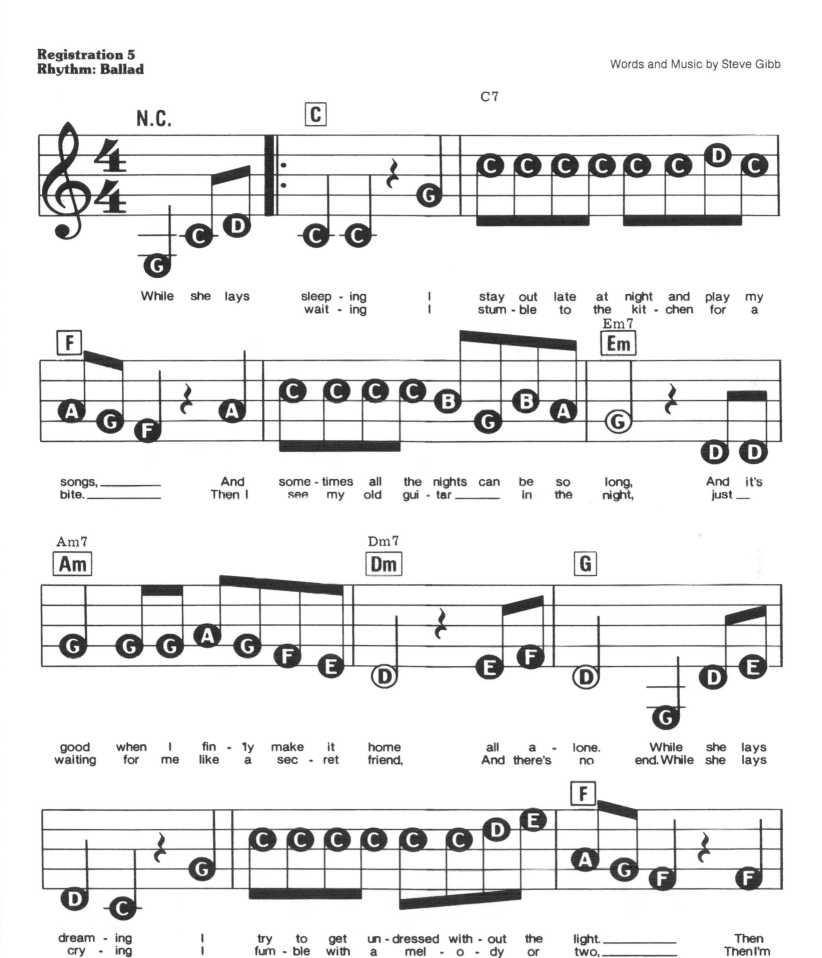

While she lays sleep - ing I stay out late at night and play my
wait - ing I stum - ble to the kit - chen for a

songs, _____ And some - times all the nights can be so long, And it's
bite. _____ Then I see my old gui - tar _____ In the night, just _____

good when I fin - 'ly make it home all a - lone. While she lays
waiting for me like a sec - ret friend, And there's no end. While she lays

dream - ing I try to get un - dressed with - out the light. _____ Then
cry - ing I fum - ble with a mel - o - dy or two, _____ Then I'm

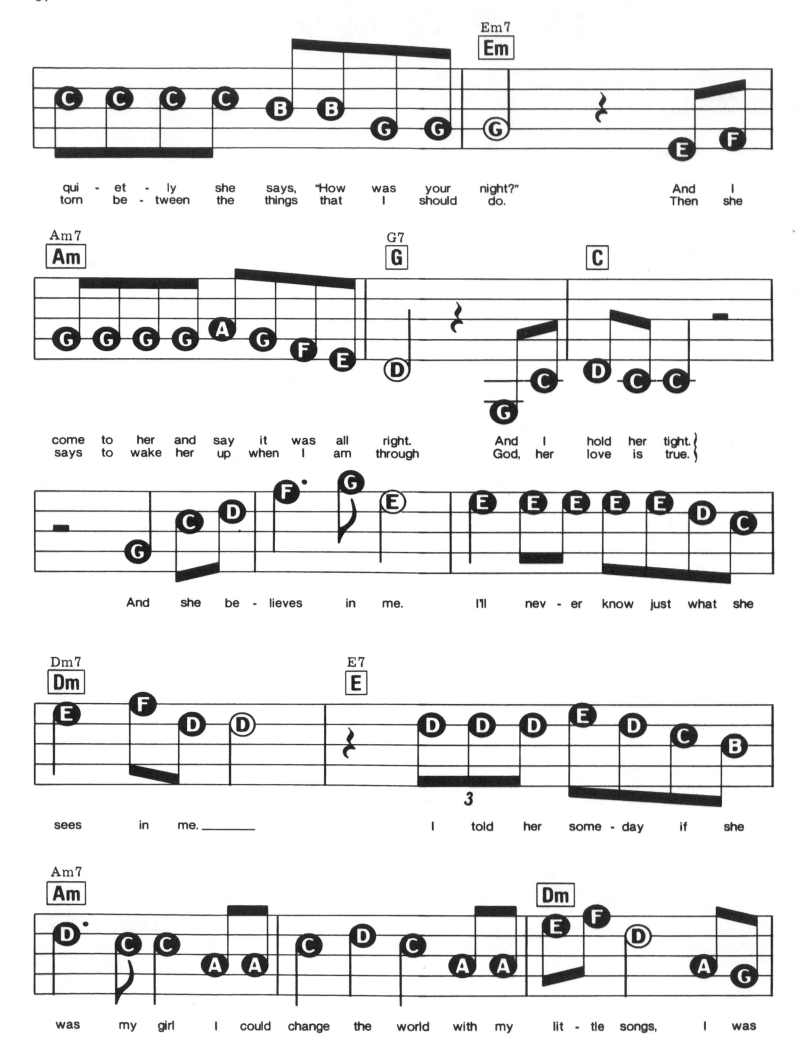

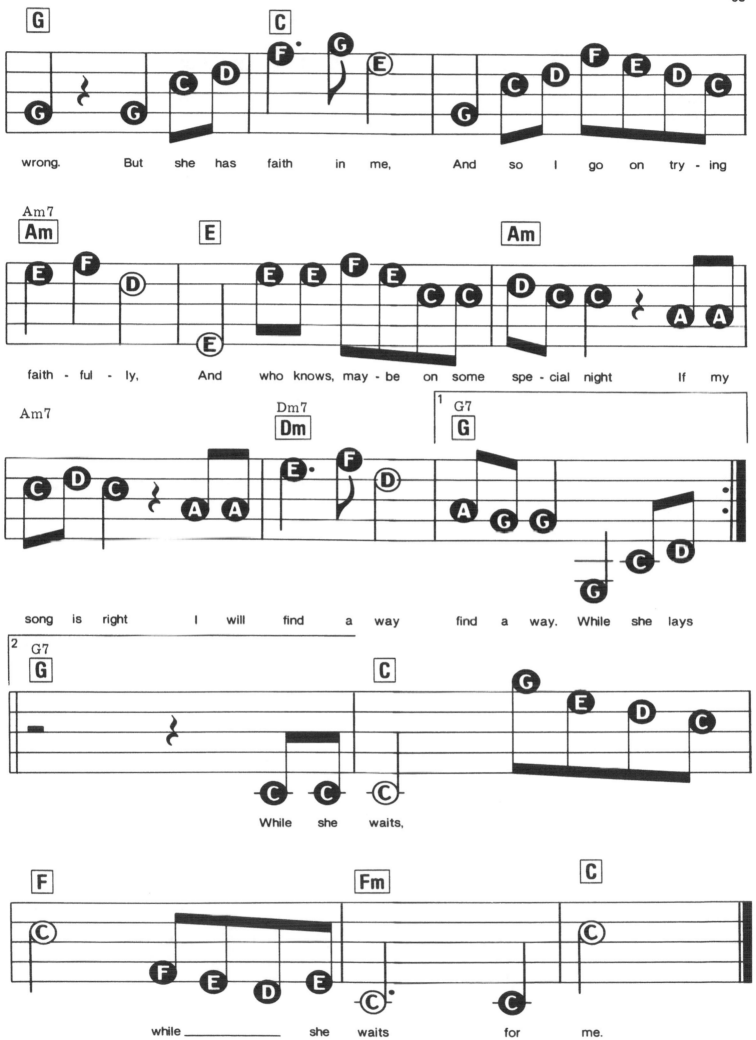

Ruby, Don't Take Your Love To Town

Registration 3
Rhythm: Swing

Words and Music by Mel Tillis

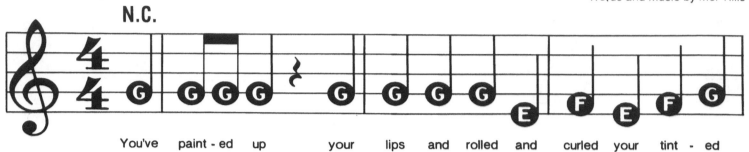

You've paint-ed up your lips and rolled and curled your tint-ed

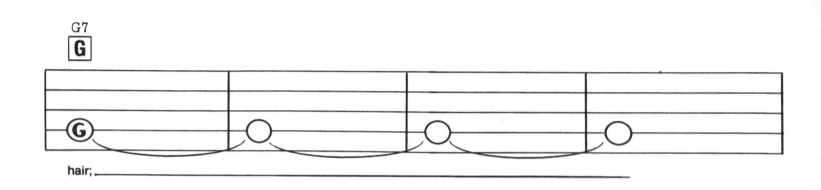

hair;

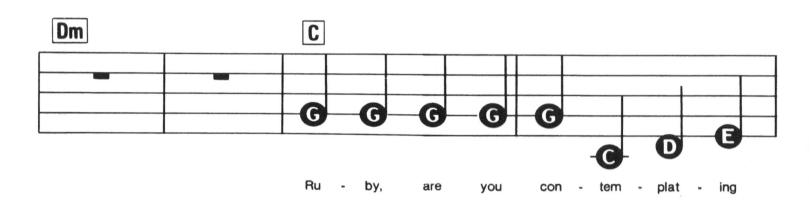

Ru - by, are you con - tem - plat - ing

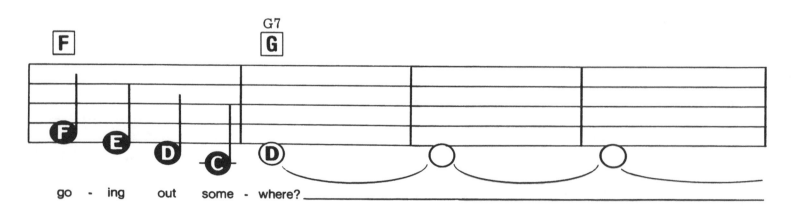

go - ing out some - where?

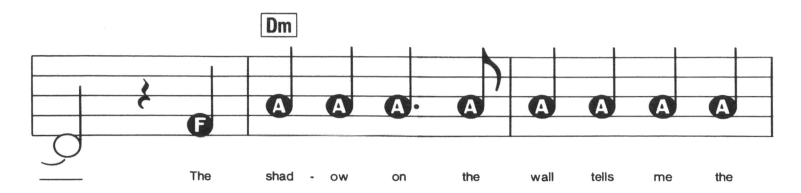

The shad - ow on the wall tells me the

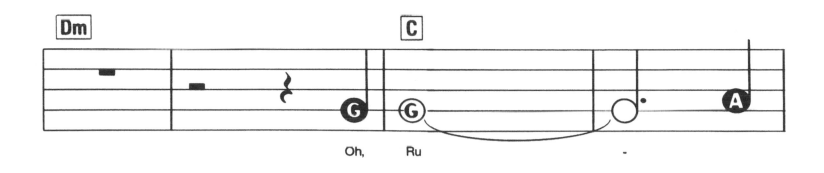

sun is go - in' down.

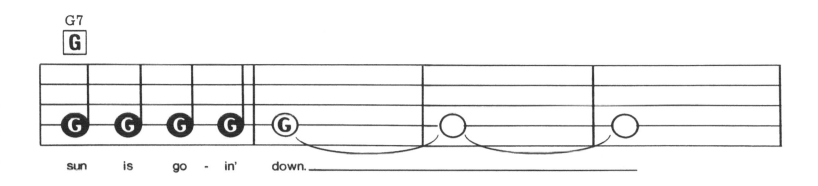

Oh, Ru -

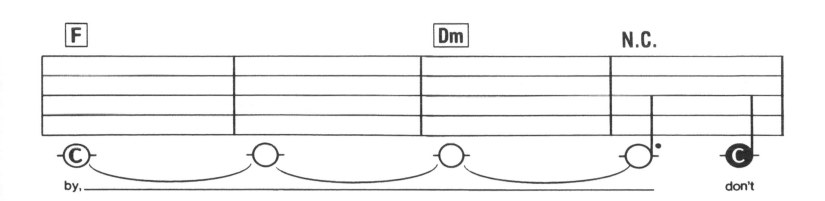

by, don't

68

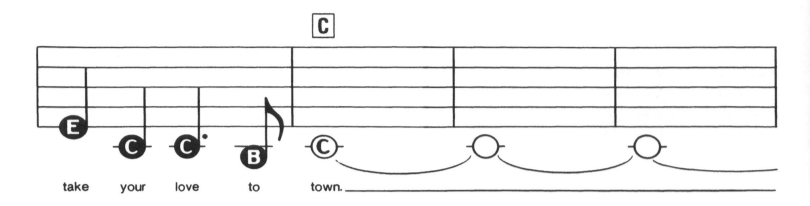

take your love to town.

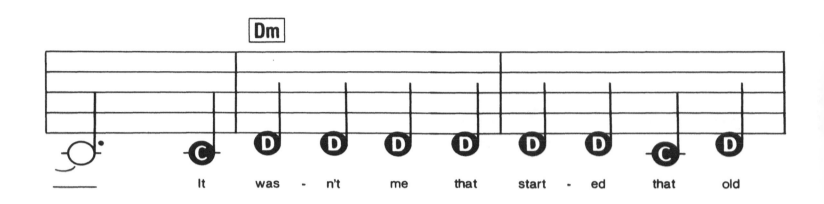

It was - n't me that start - ed that old

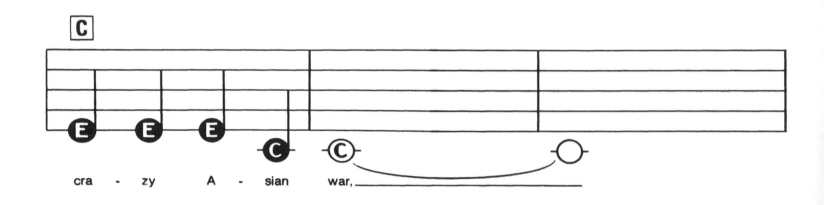

cra - zy A - sian war,

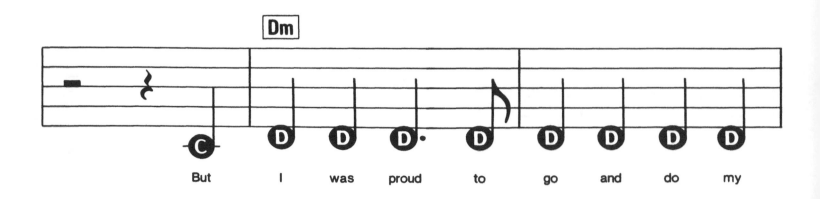

But I was proud to go and do my

69

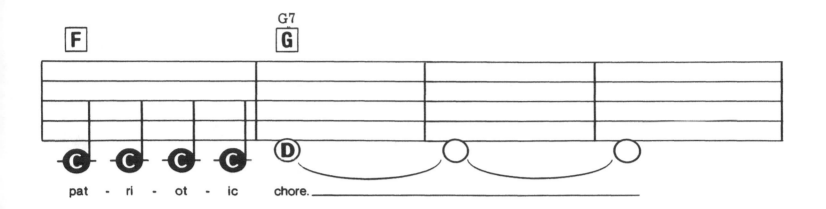

pat - ri - ot - ic   chore.

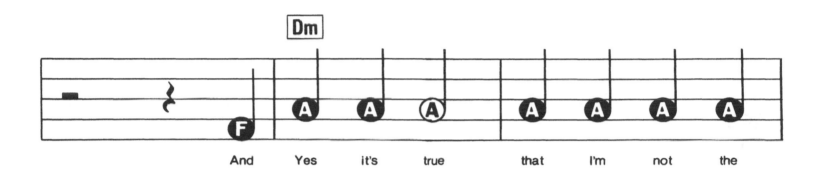

And   Yes   it's   true   that   I'm   not   the

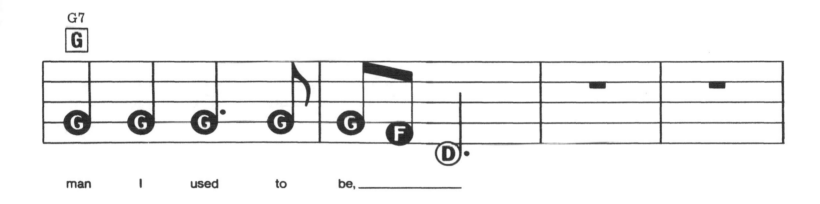

man   I   used   to   be,

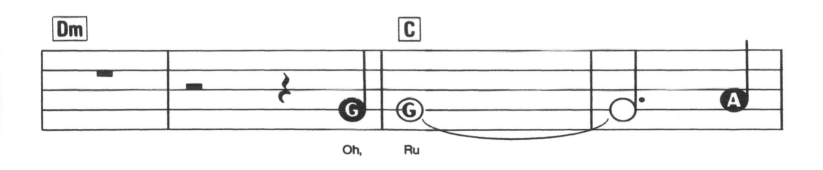

Oh,   Ru

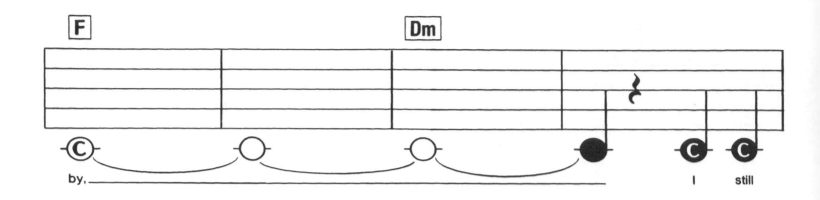

by,

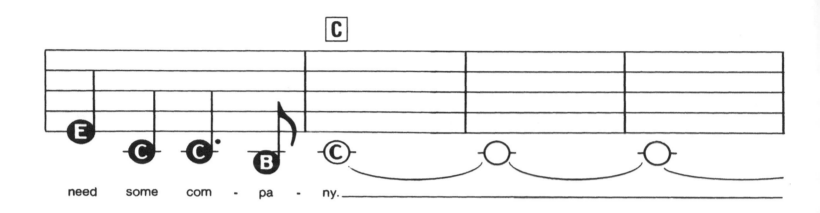

need some com - pa - ny.

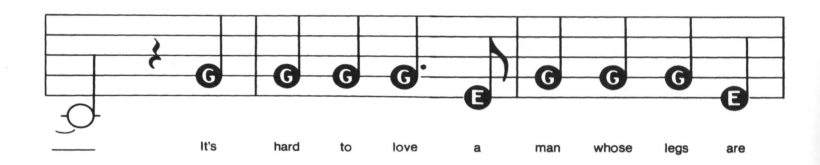

It's hard to love a man whose legs are

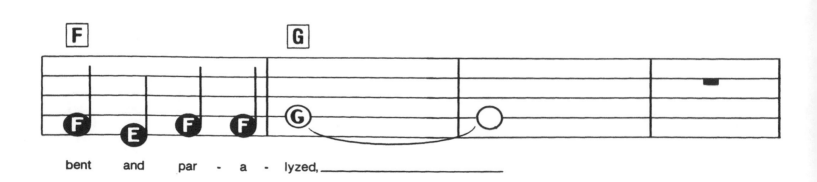

bent and par - a - lyzed,

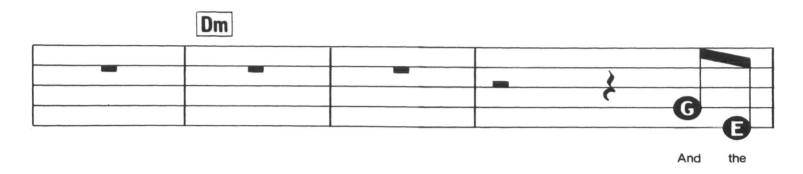

And the

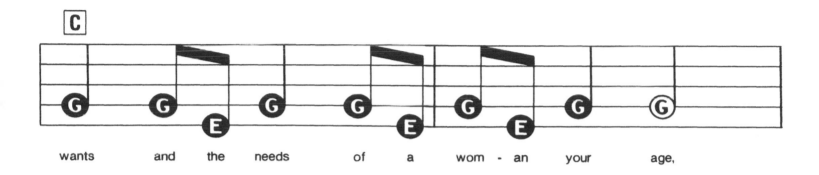

wants and the needs of a wom - an your age,

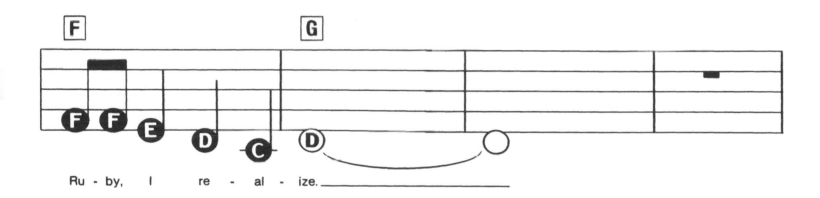

Ru - by, I re - al - ize._____

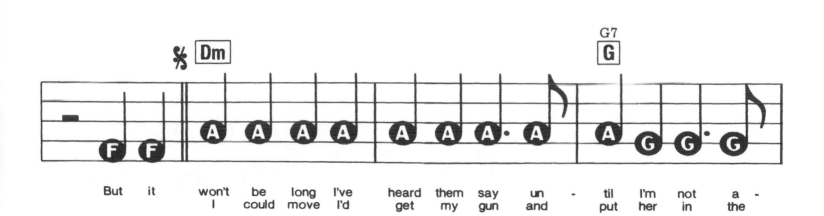

But it won't be long I've heard them say un - til I'm not a -
I could move I'd get my gun and put her in the

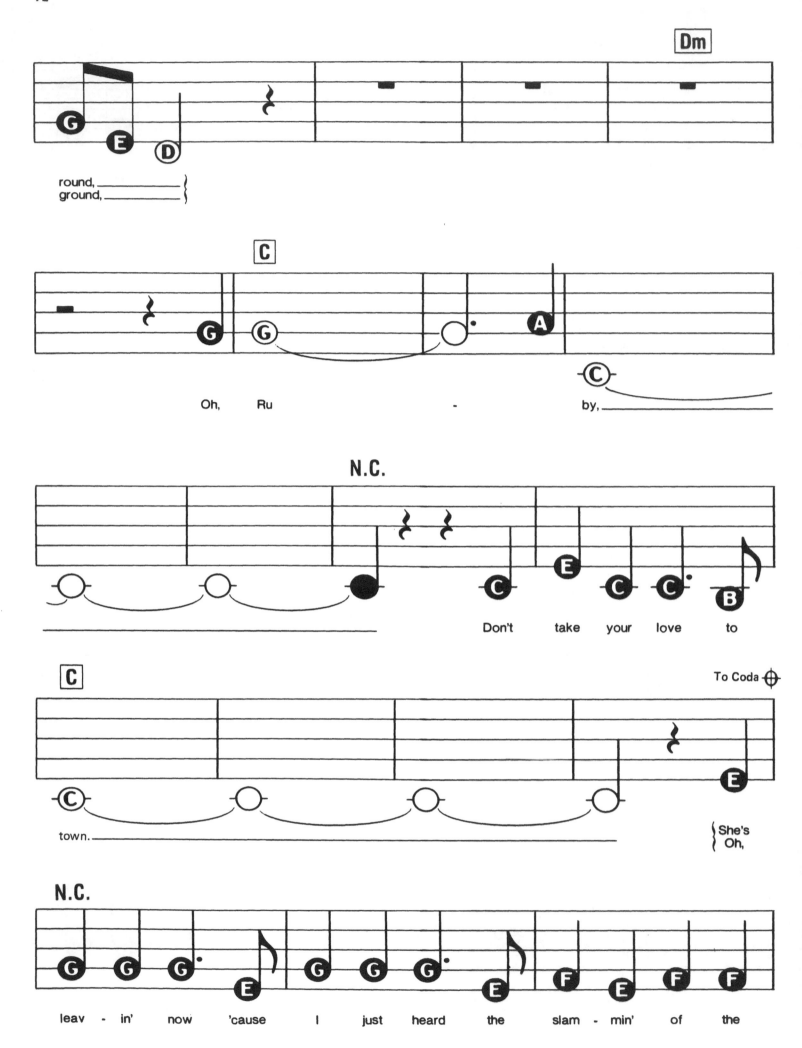

door,

The

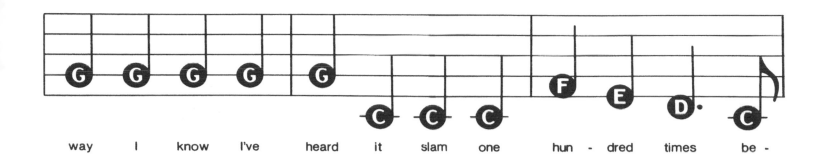

way I know I've heard it slam one hun - dred times be -

D.S. al Coda
(Return to 𝄋
Play to ⊕ and
skip to Coda)

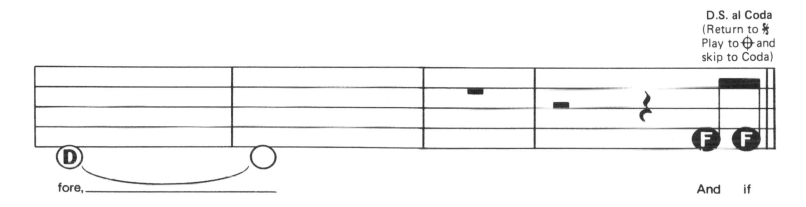

fore,_____

And if

CODA

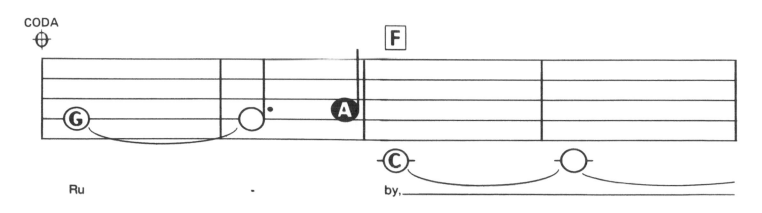

Ru - by,_____

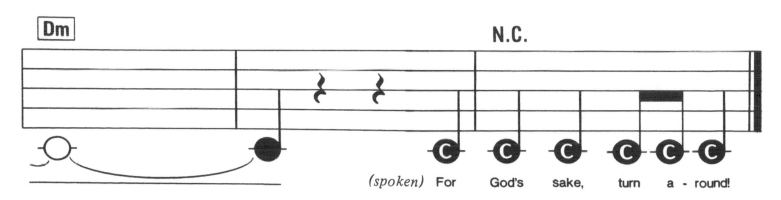

(spoken) For God's sake, turn a - round!

Reuben James

Registration 7
Rhythm: Country Western

Words and Music by Alex Harvey
and Barry Etris

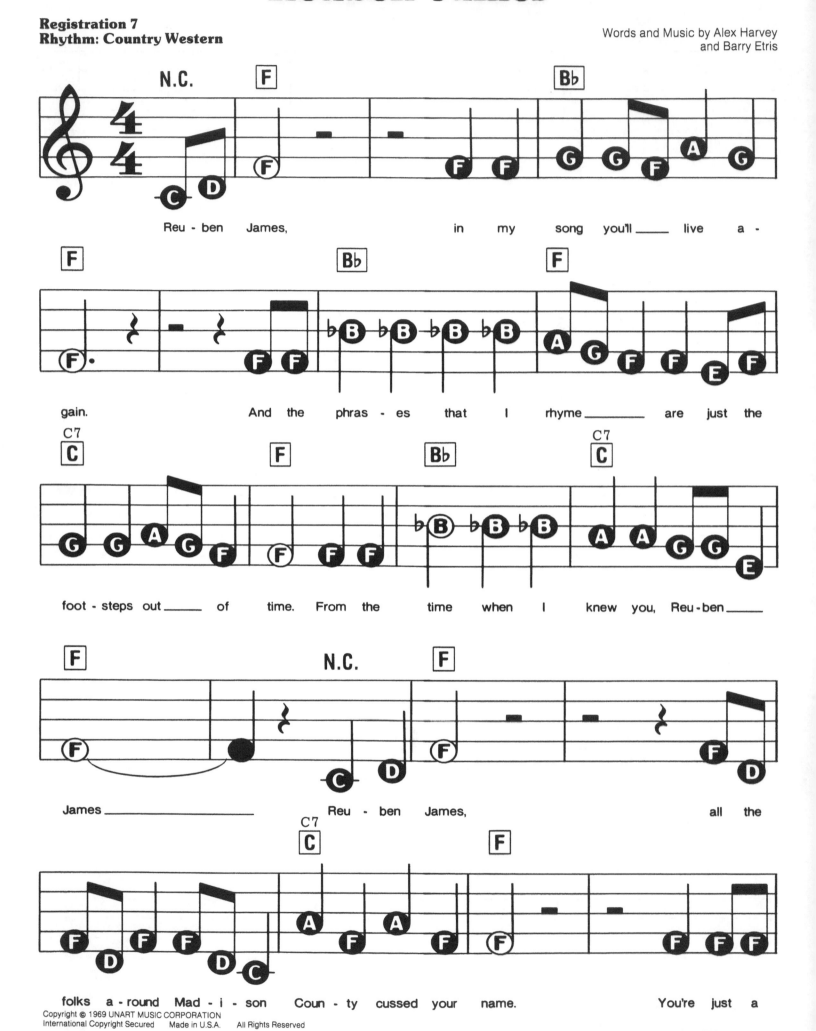

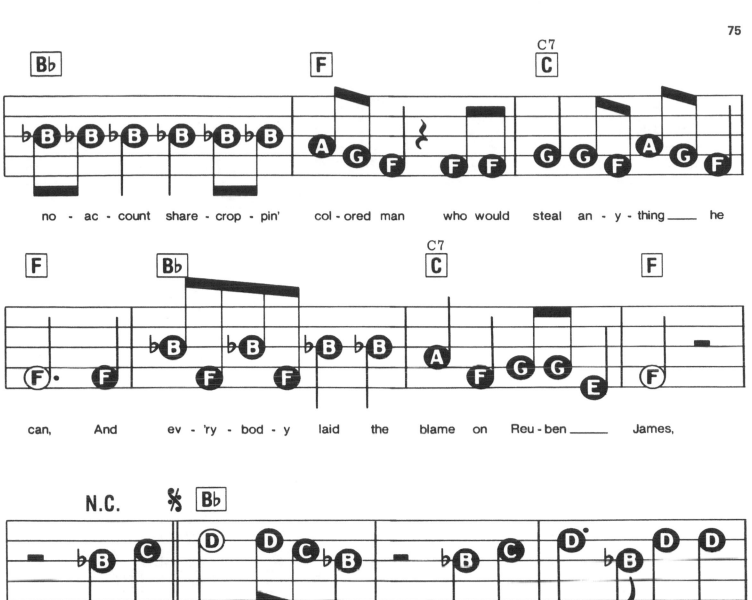

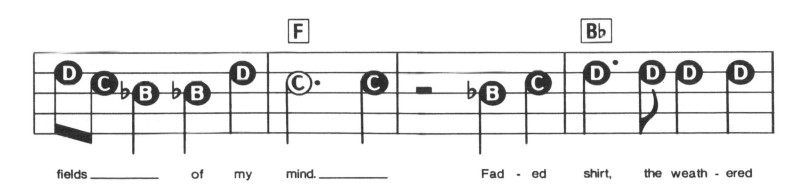

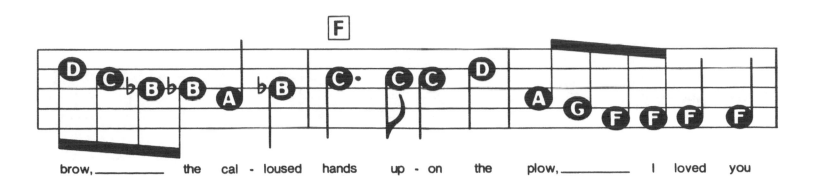

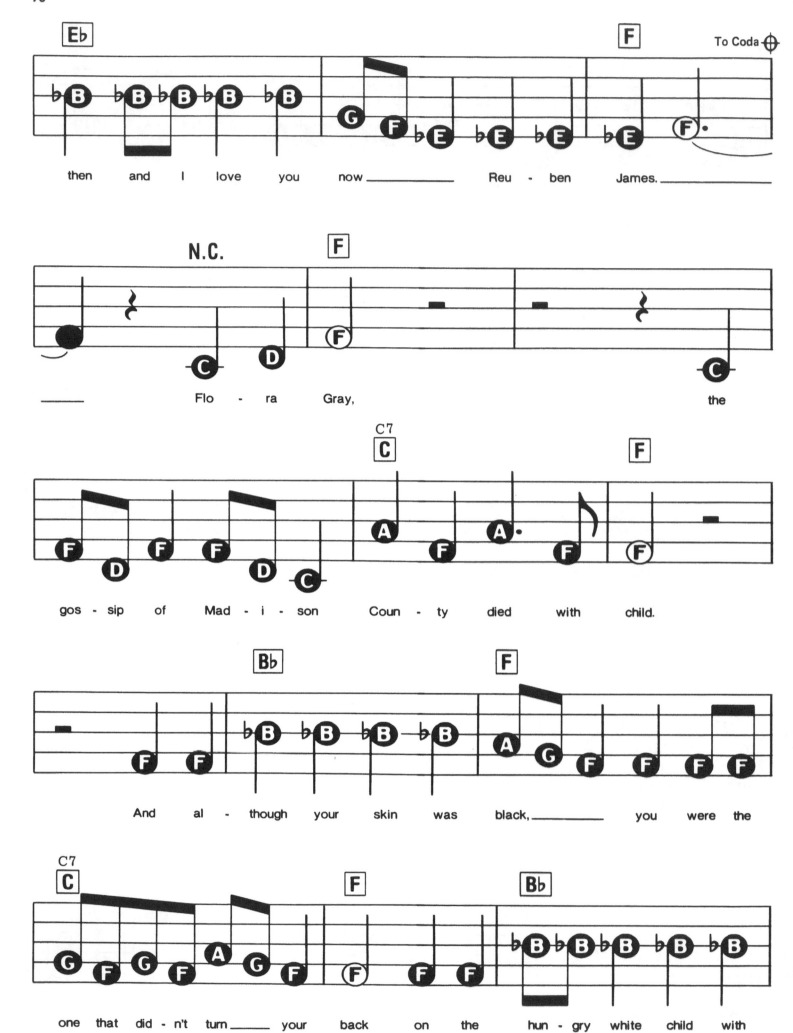

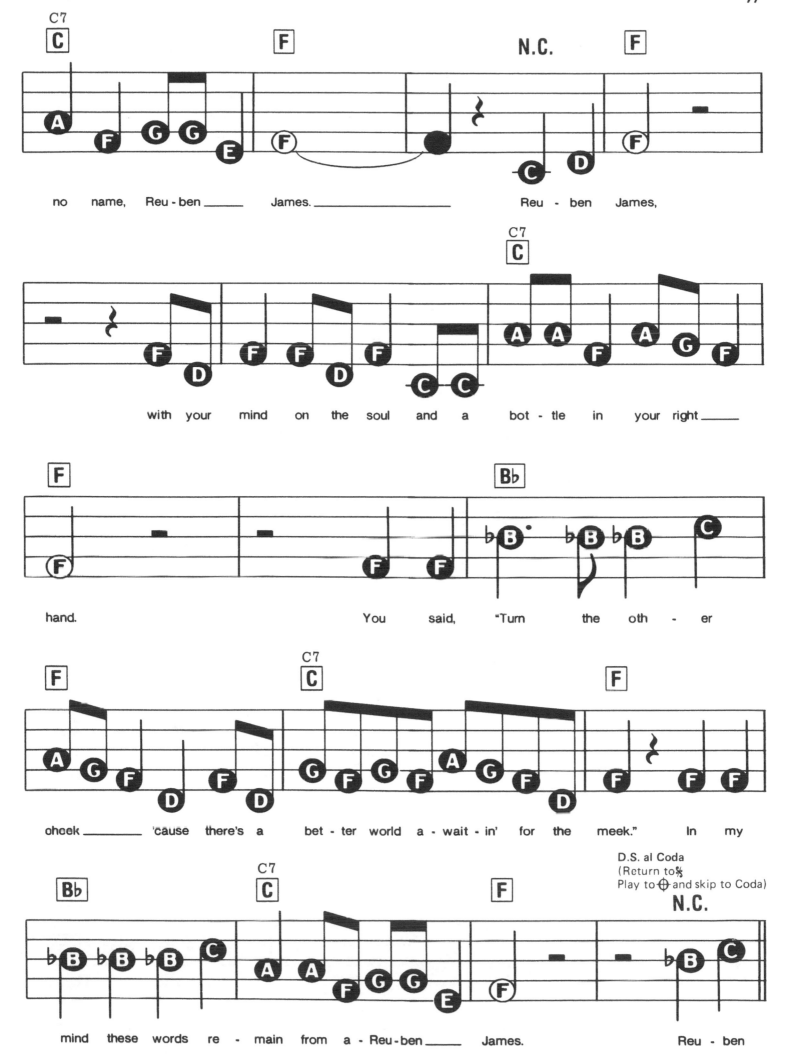

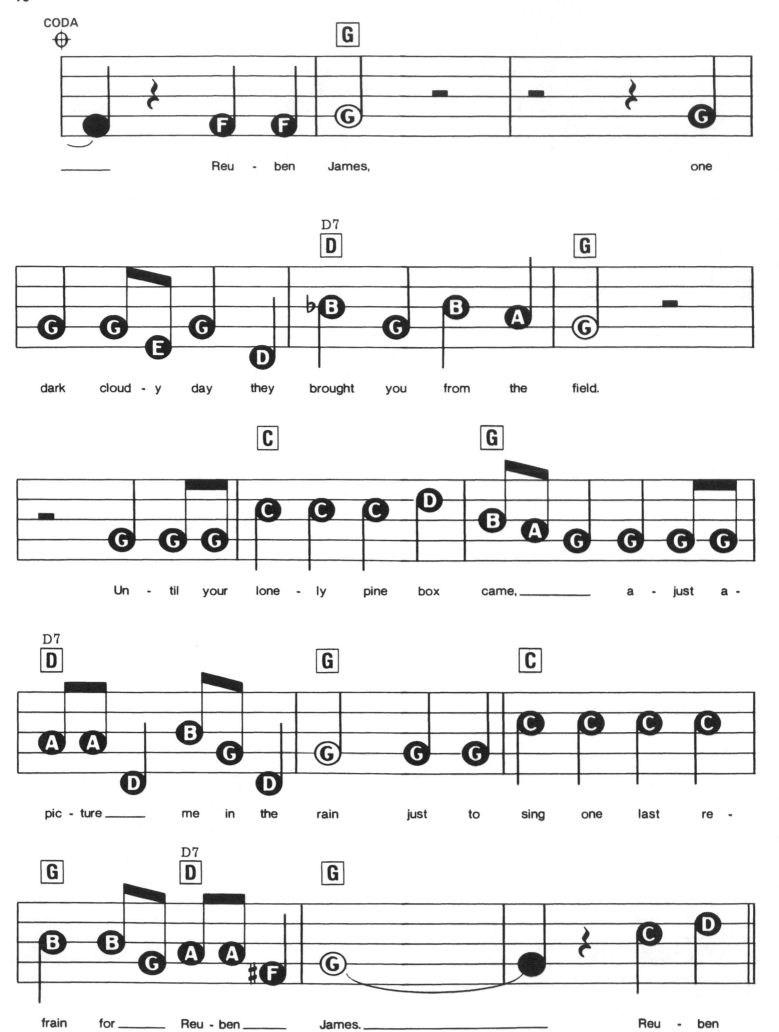

79

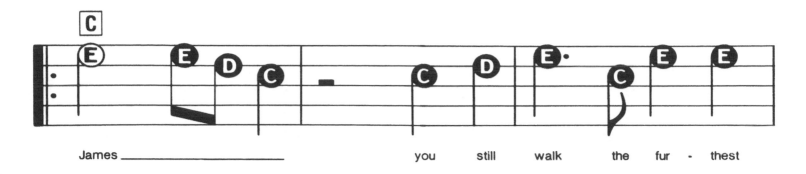

James _____ you still walk the fur - thest

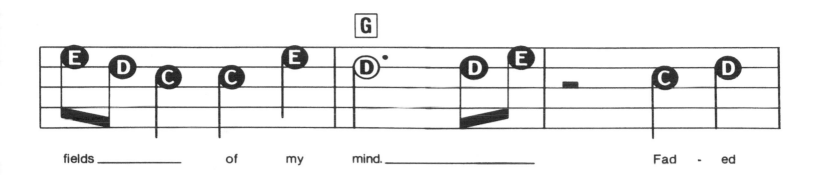

fields _____ of my mind. _____ Fad - ed

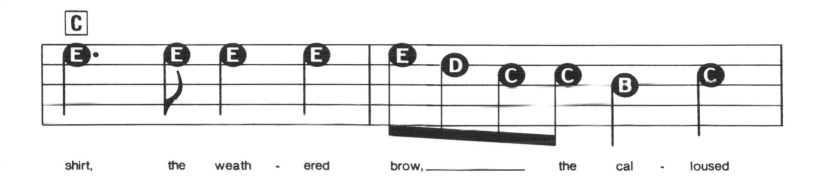

shirt, the weath - ered brow, _____ the cal - loused

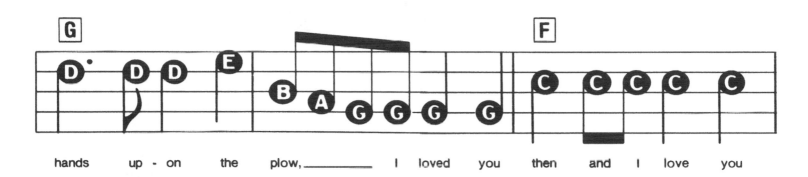

hands up - on the plow, _____ I loved you then and I love you

Repeat and Fade

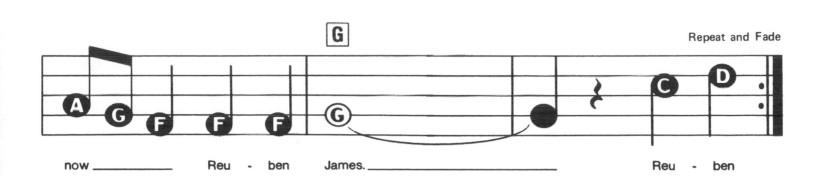

now _____ Reu - ben James. _____ Reu - ben

Love Or Something Like It

Registration 5
Rhythm: Country Western

Words and Music by Kenny Rogers
and Steve Glassmeyer

Show me a bar with _____ a good look - ing wom - an, _____
That's when I asked her _____ "My place or your _____ place?

then just get out of my way.
I hope I'm not out of line."

Turn on the juke - box, _____ I'll
I asked the wrong thing _____ to

show you a song you should play. _____
just the a right wom - an this time. _____

Soon - er or lat - er _____ a few shots of bour - bon, _____
She knew a ho - tel, _____ she e - ven had a name we could

81

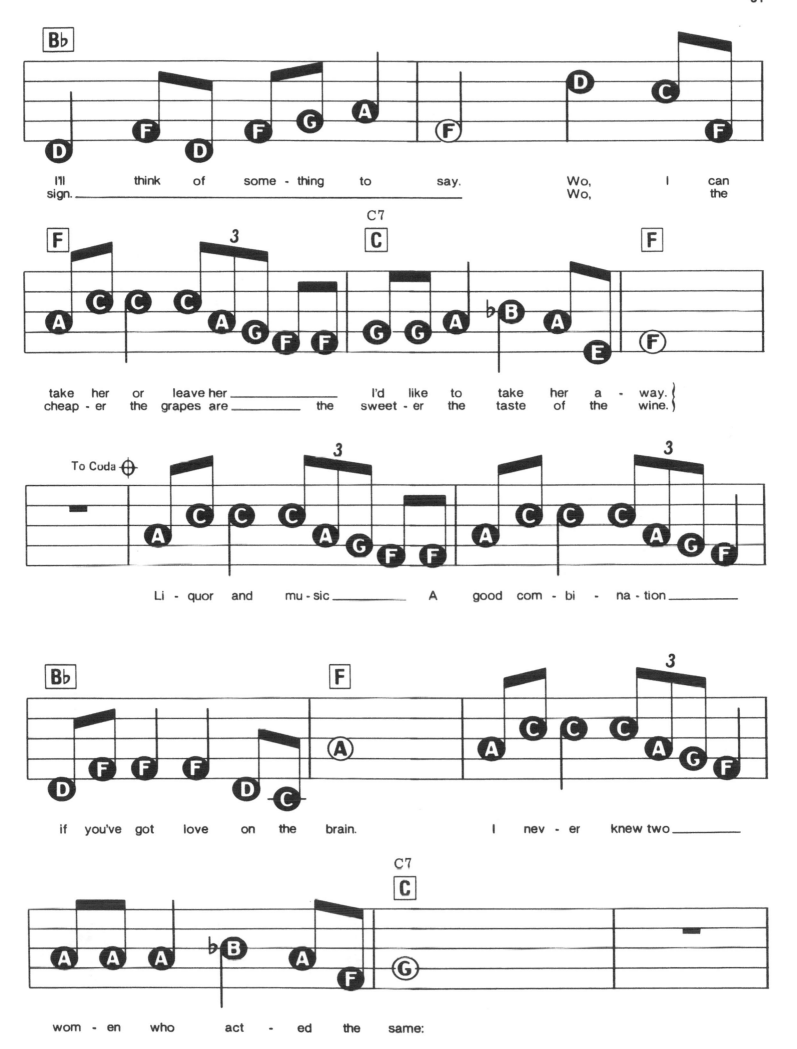

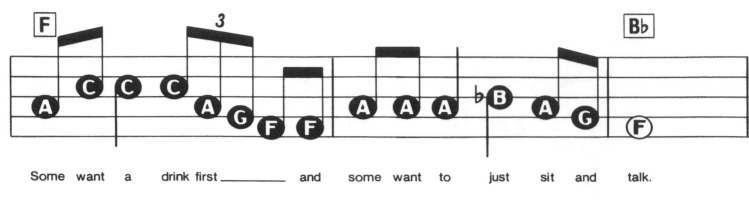

Some want a drink first _____ and some want to just sit and talk.

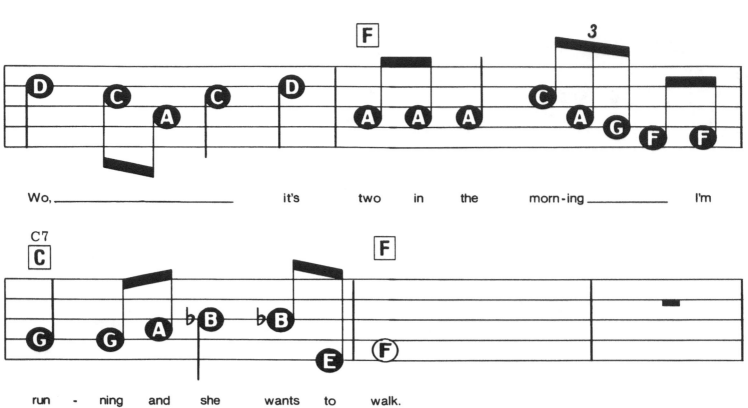

Wo, _____ it's two in the morn-ing _____ I'm

run - ning and she wants to walk.

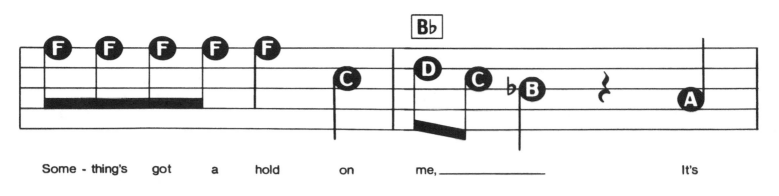

Some - thing's got a hold on me, _____ It's

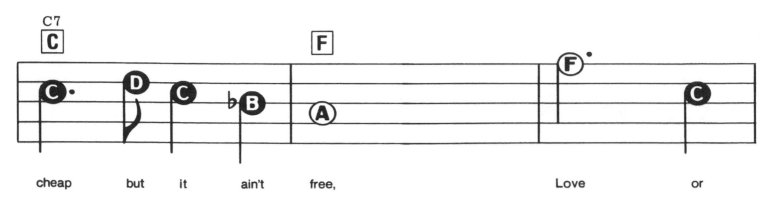

cheap but it ain't free, Love or

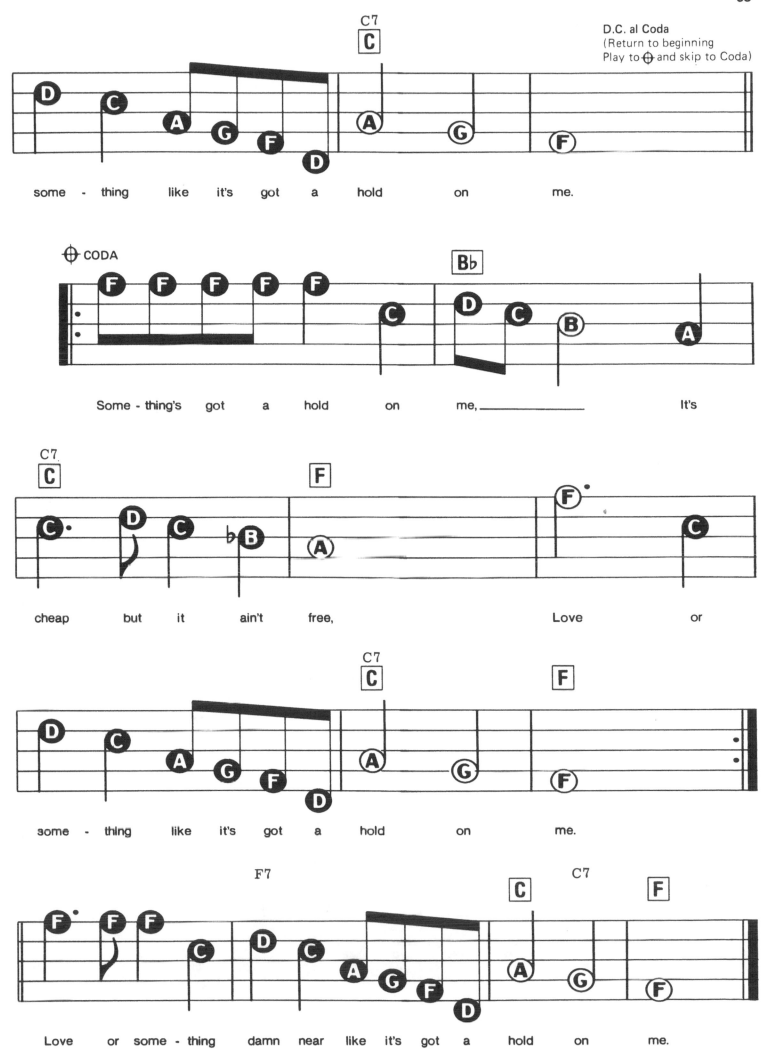

So In Love With You

Registration 1
Rhythm: Ballad

Words and Music by Lionel Richie

Girl, I'll sing you love songs ev - 'ry morn - in,
Come on sing girl, I need you here be - side me,
You're the one that keeps me all to - geth - er,

By my side you'll nev - er be a -
Let I'll show me hold you love like you've nev -
me you in my arms all through er
the

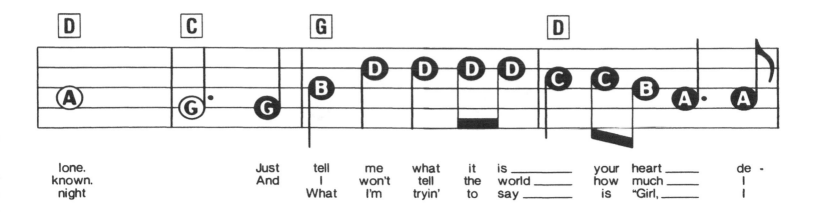

lone.
known.
night

Just tell me what it is _____ your heart _____ de-
And I won't tell the world _____ how much _____ I
What I'm tryin' to say _____ is "Girl, _____ I

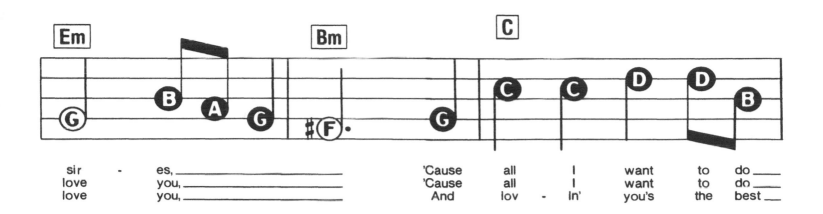

sir - es, _____
love you, _____
love you, _____

'Cause all I want to do ___
'Cause all I want to do ___
And lov - in' you's the best ___

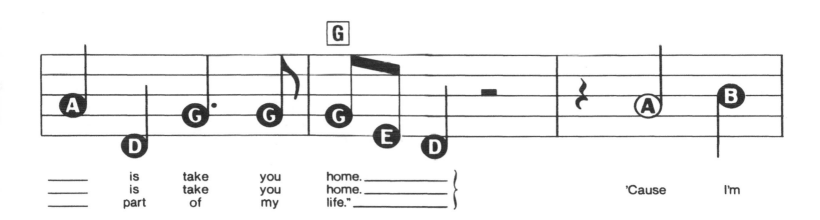

_____ is take you home. _____
_____ is take you home. _____
_____ part of my life." _____

'Cause I'm

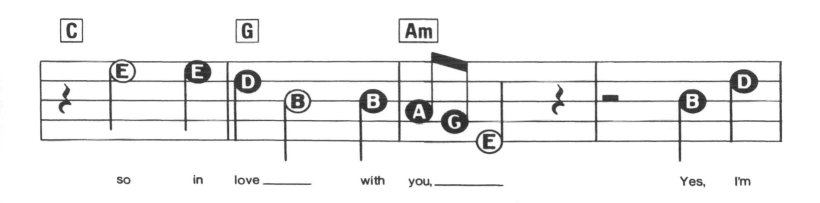

so in love _____ with you, _____

Yes, I'm

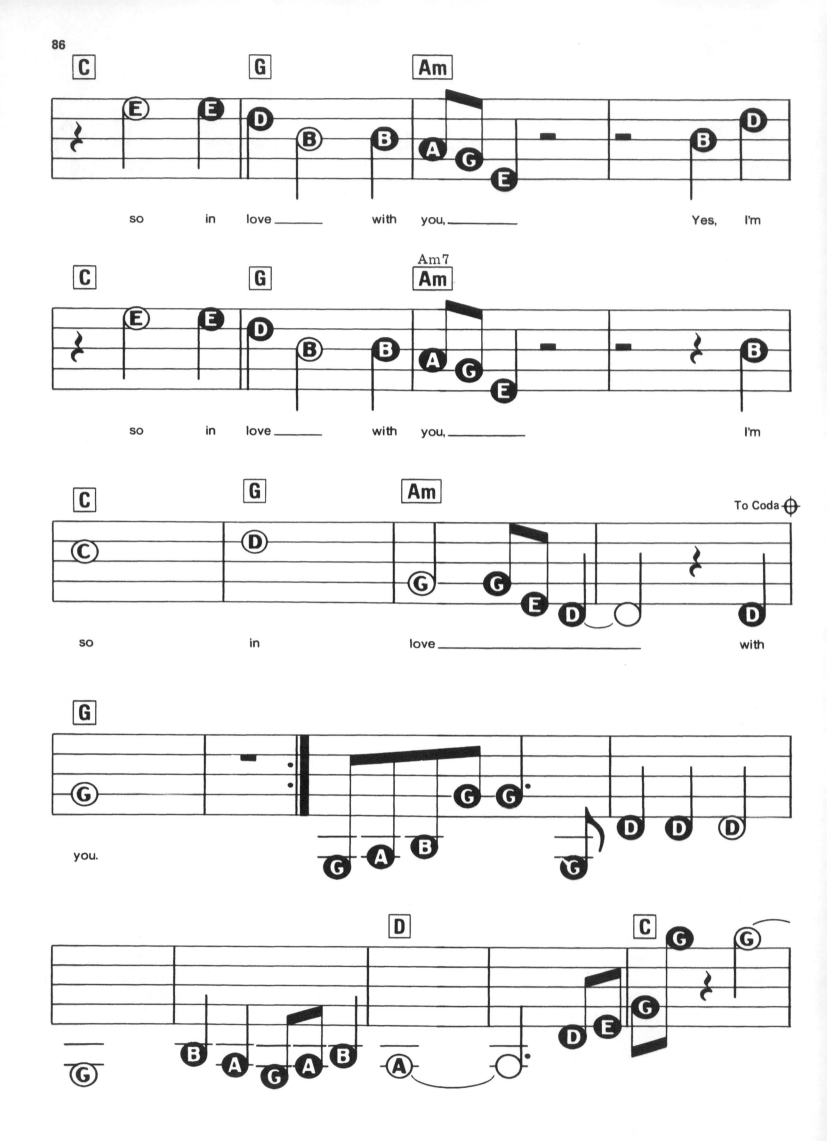

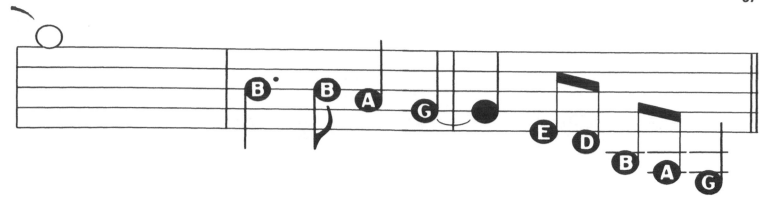

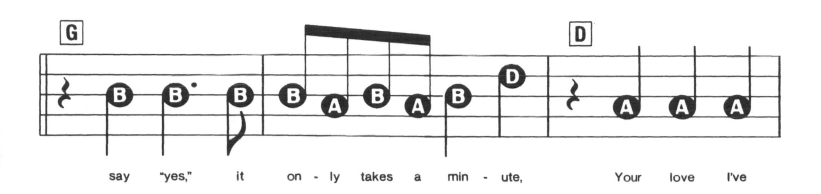

say "yes," it on - ly takes a min - ute, Your love I've

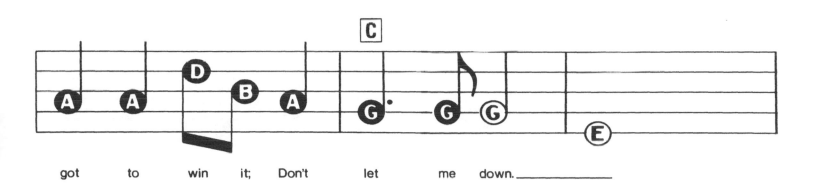

got to win it; Don't let me down._____

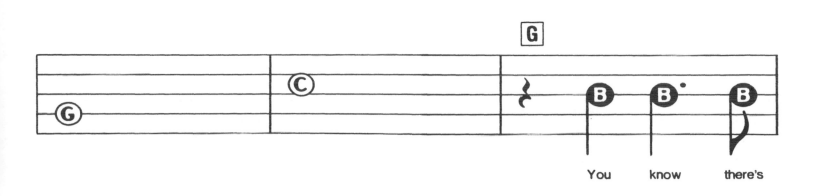

You know there's

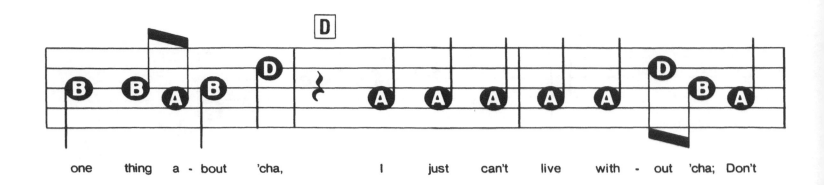

one thing a - bout 'cha, I just can't live with - out 'cha; Don't

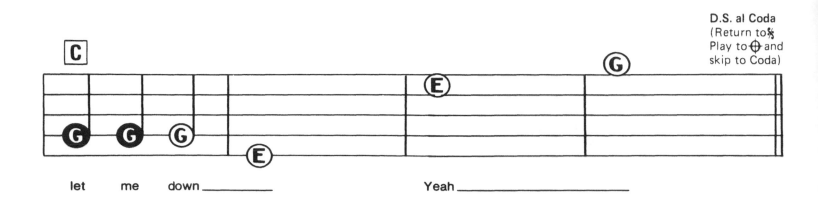

D.S. al Coda
(Return to %
Play to ⊕ and
skip to Coda)

let me down _____ Yeah _____

⊕ CODA

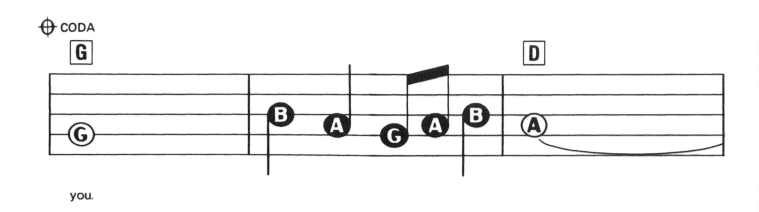

you.

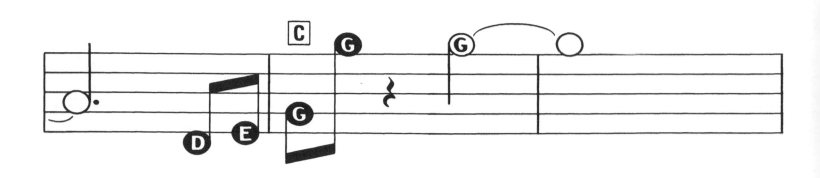

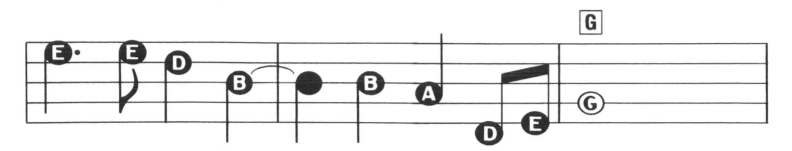

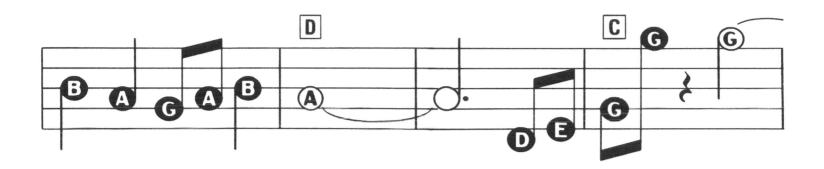

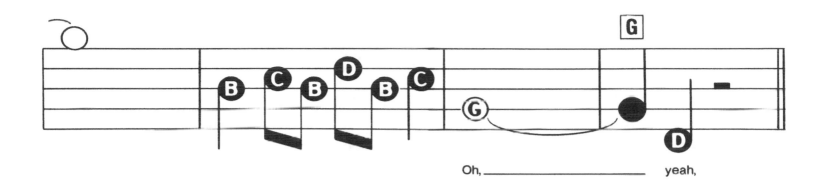

Oh, _____ yeah,

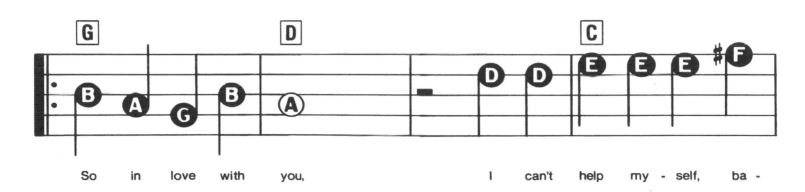

So in love with you, I can't help my-self, ba -

Repeat and Fade

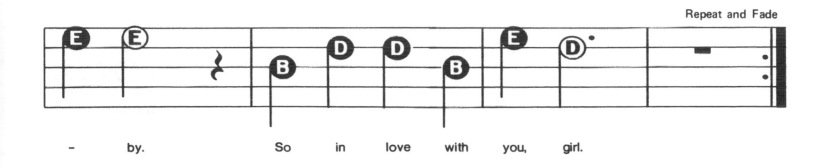

- by. So in love with you, girl.

Sweet Music Man

Registration 5
Rhythm: Country Western

Words and Music by Kenny Rogers

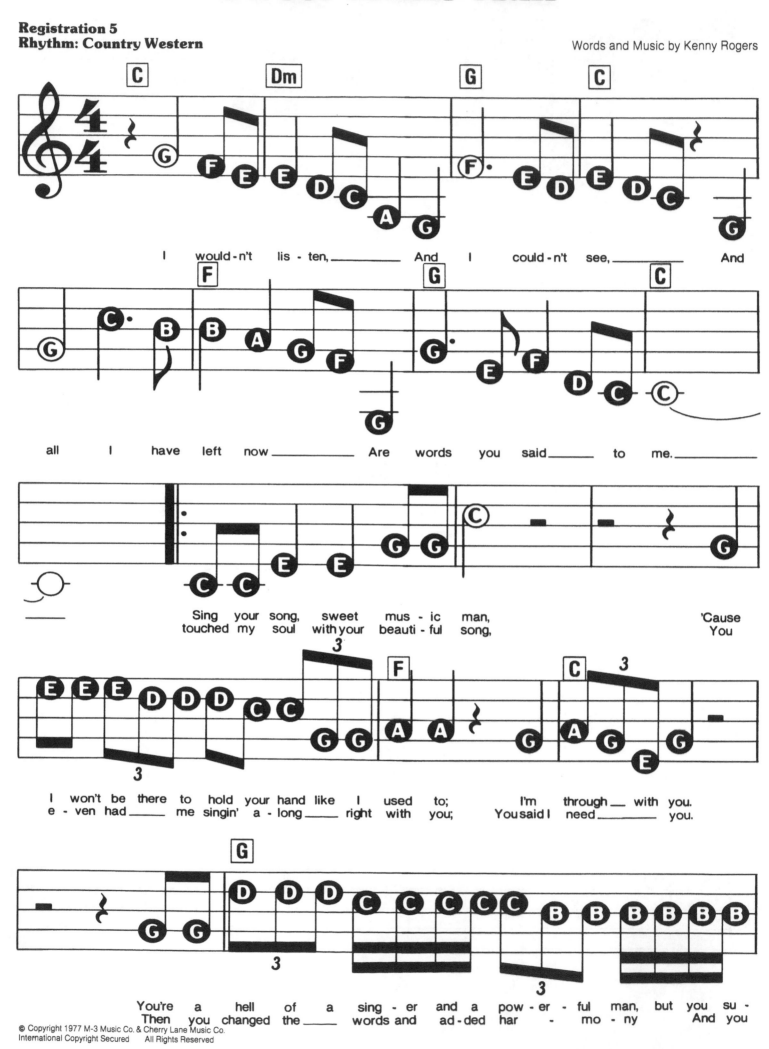

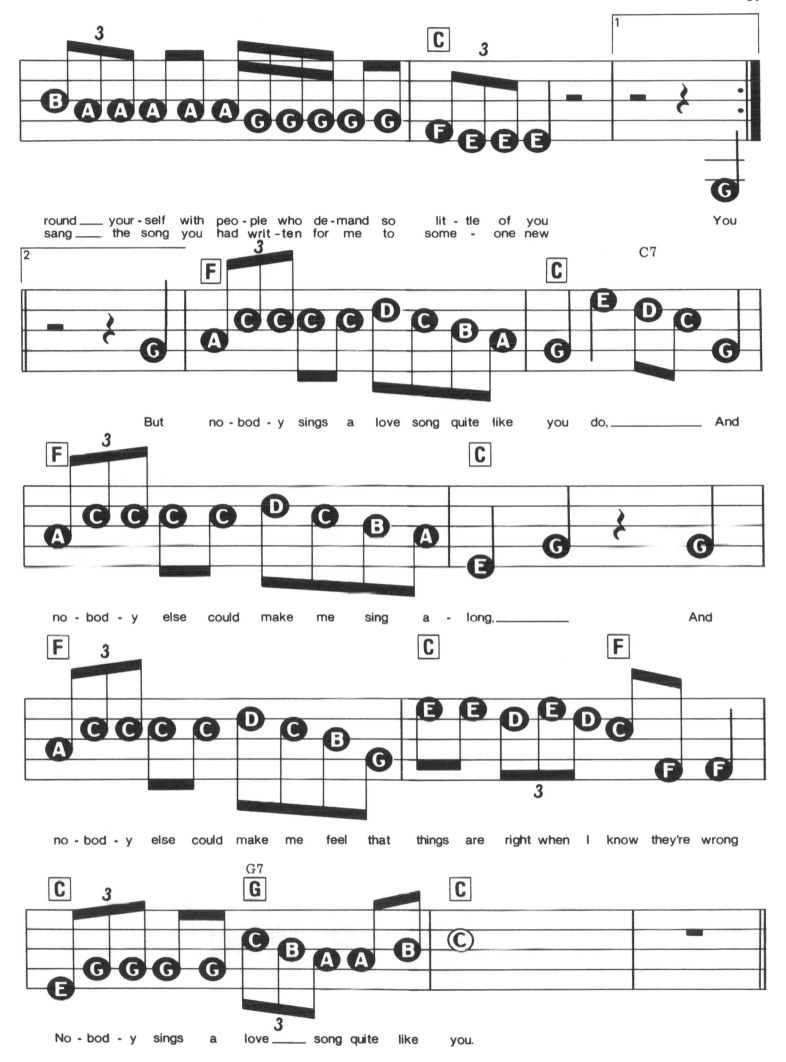

92

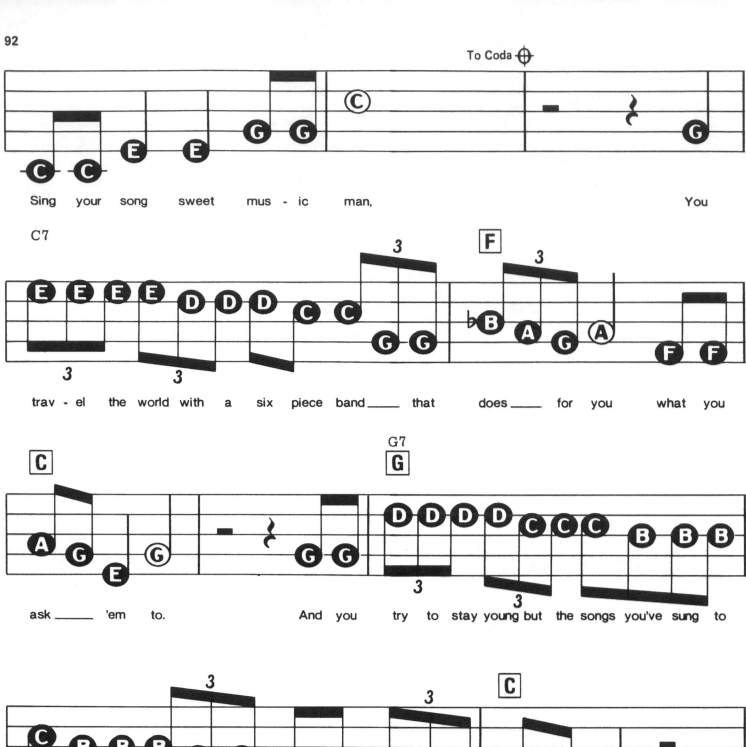

To Coda ⊕

Sing your song sweet mus - ic man, You

C7

trav - el the world with a six piece band____ that does ____ for you what you

C   G7 G

ask ____ 'em to.   And you try to stay young but the songs you've sung to

C

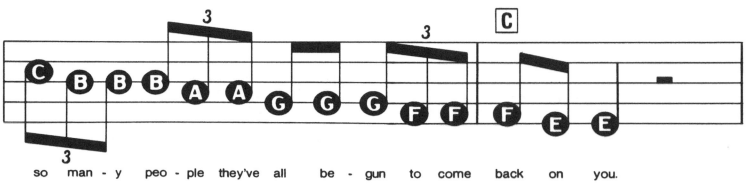

so man - y peo - ple they've all be - gun to come back on you.

So sing your song, sad mus - ic man,

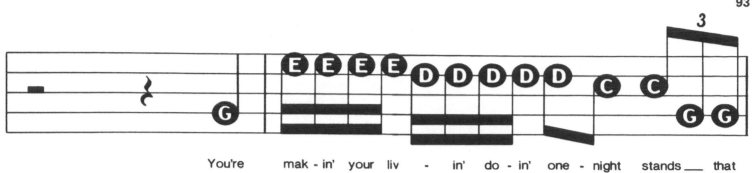

You're mak-in' your liv - in' do-in' one - night stands __ that

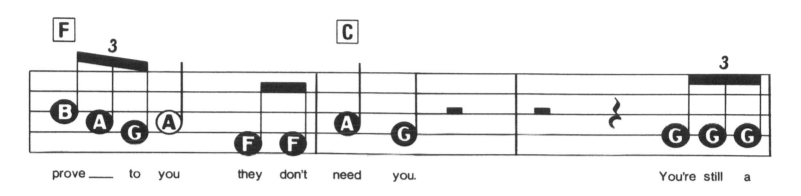

prove __ to you they don't need you. You're still a

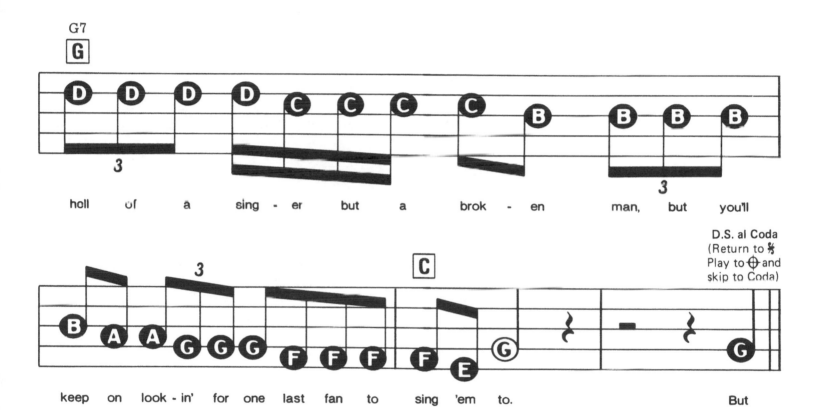

G7

holl of a sing - er but a brok - en man, but you'll

D.S. al Coda
(Return to %
Play to ⊕ and
skip to Coda)

keep on look-in' for one last fan to sing 'em to. But

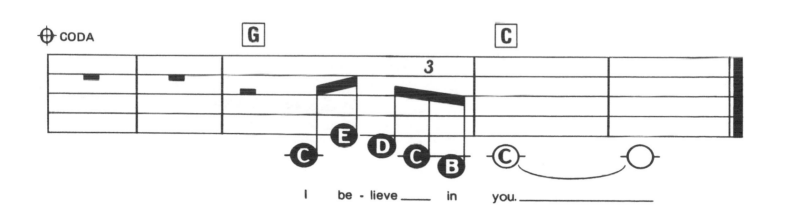

⊕ CODA

I be - lieve __ in you. _____

A Love Song

Registration 10
Rhythm: Swing

Words and Music by Lee Greenwood

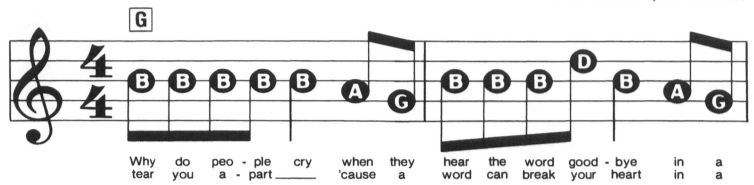

Why do peo - ple cry when they hear the word good - bye in a
tear you a - part _____ 'cause a word can break your heart in a

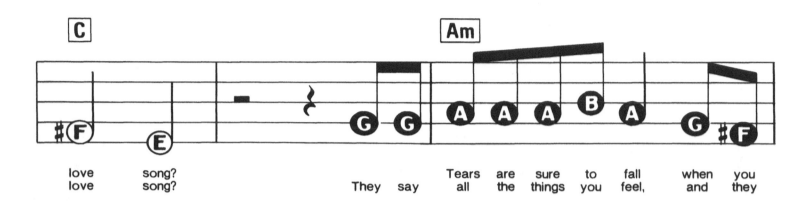

love song?
love song?
They say Tears are sure to fall when you
all the things you feel, and they

know they gave it all in a love song.
make it sound so real in a love song.
Some - how two
It seems that

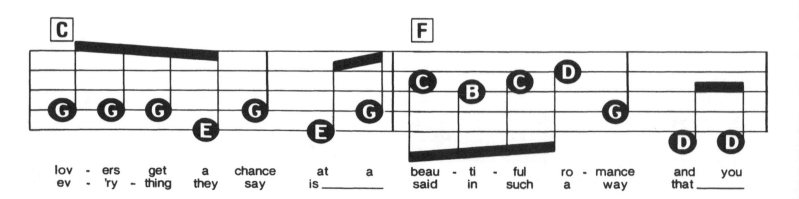

lov - ers get a chance at a beau - ti - ful ro - mance and you
ev - 'ry - thing they say is _____ said in such a way that _____

95

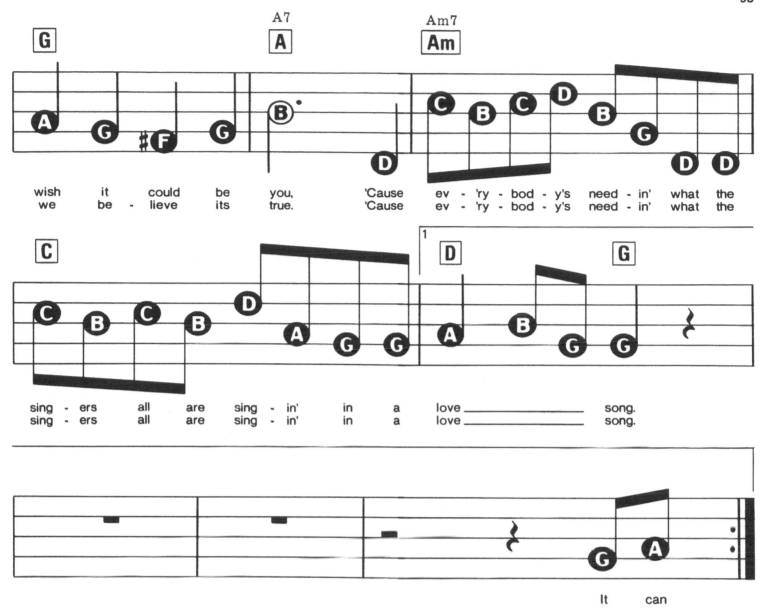

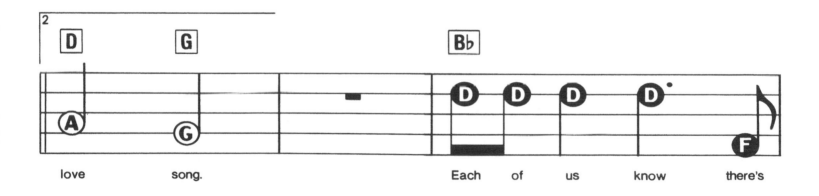

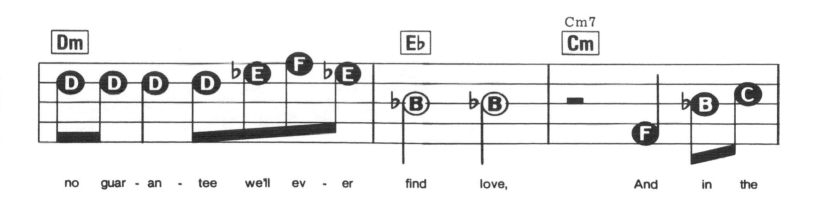

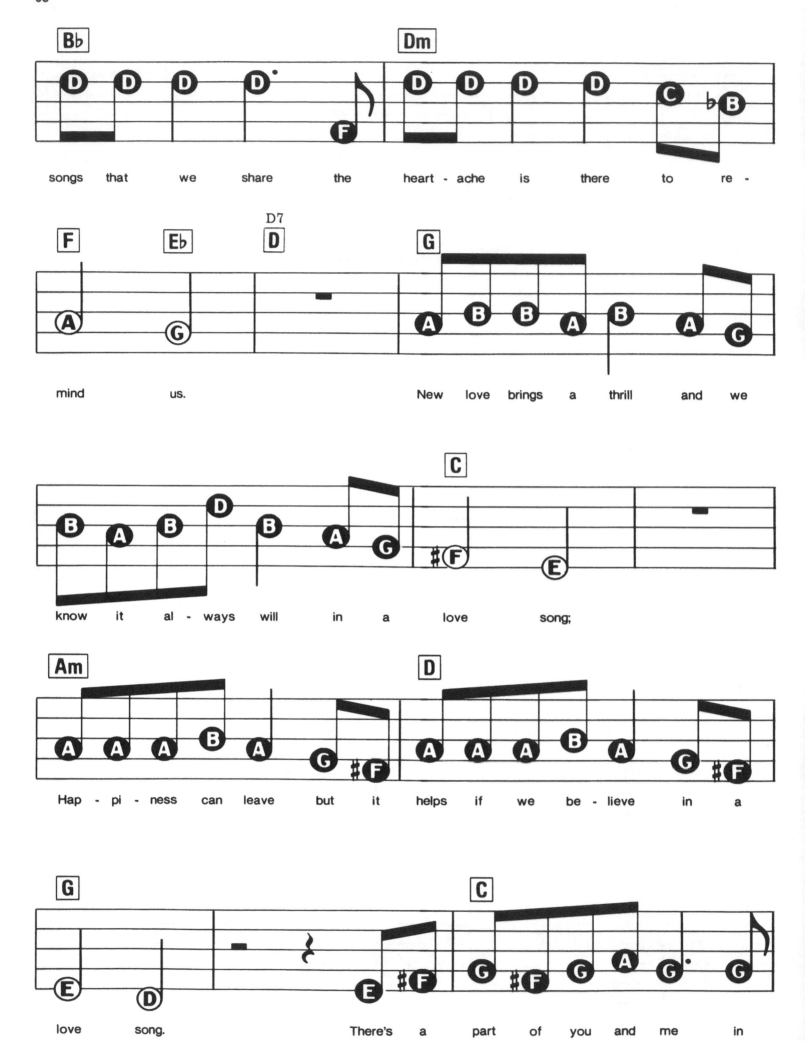

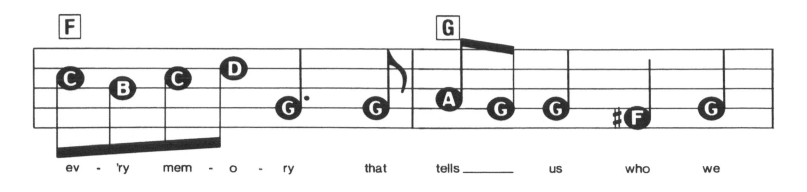

ev - 'ry mem - o - ry that tells _____ us who we

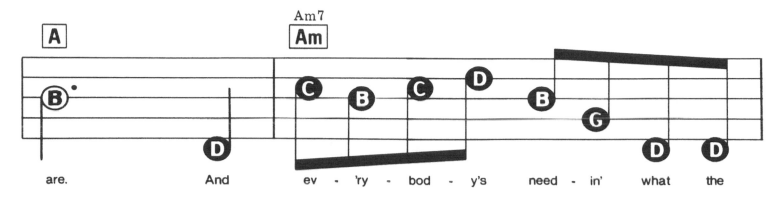

are. And ev - 'ry - bod - y's need - in' what the

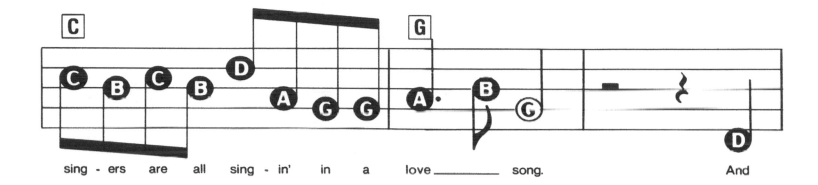

sing - ers are all sing - in' in a love _____ song. And

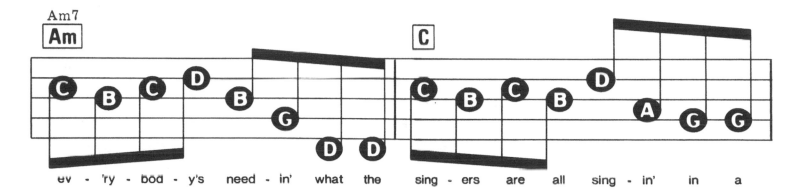

ev - 'ry - bod - y's need - in' what the sing - ers are all sing - in' in a

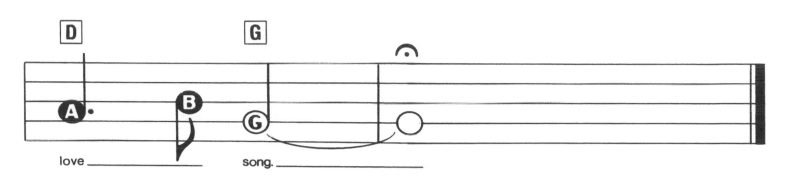

love _____ song. _____

98

Making Music For Money

Registration 4
Rhythm: Swing

Words and Music by Alex Harvey

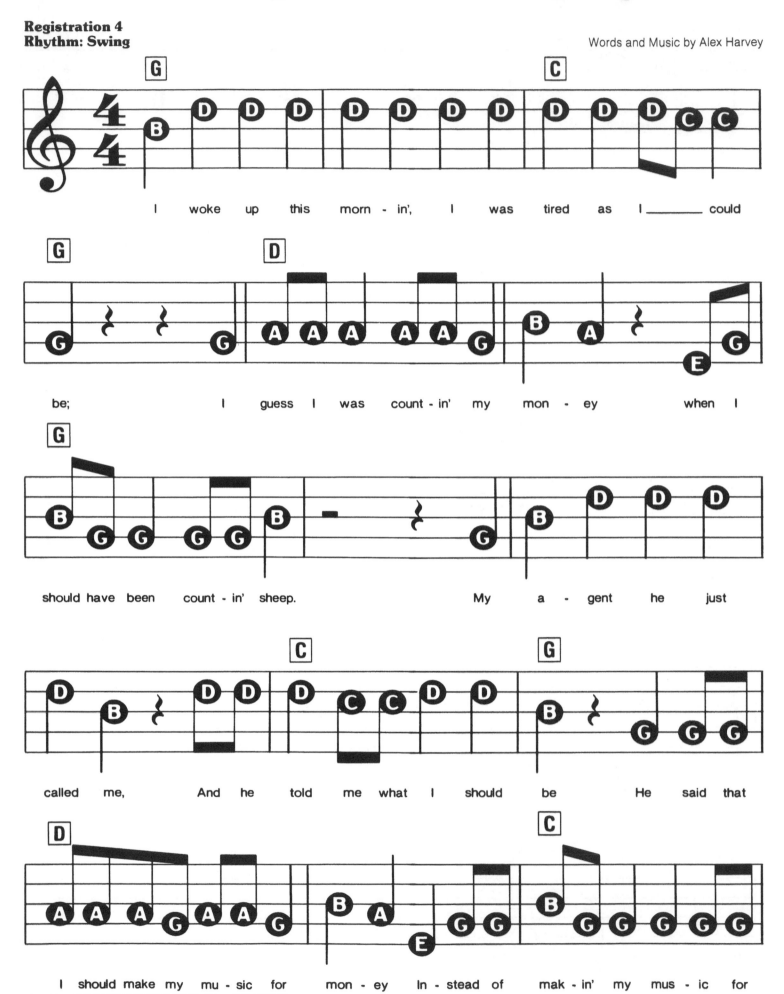

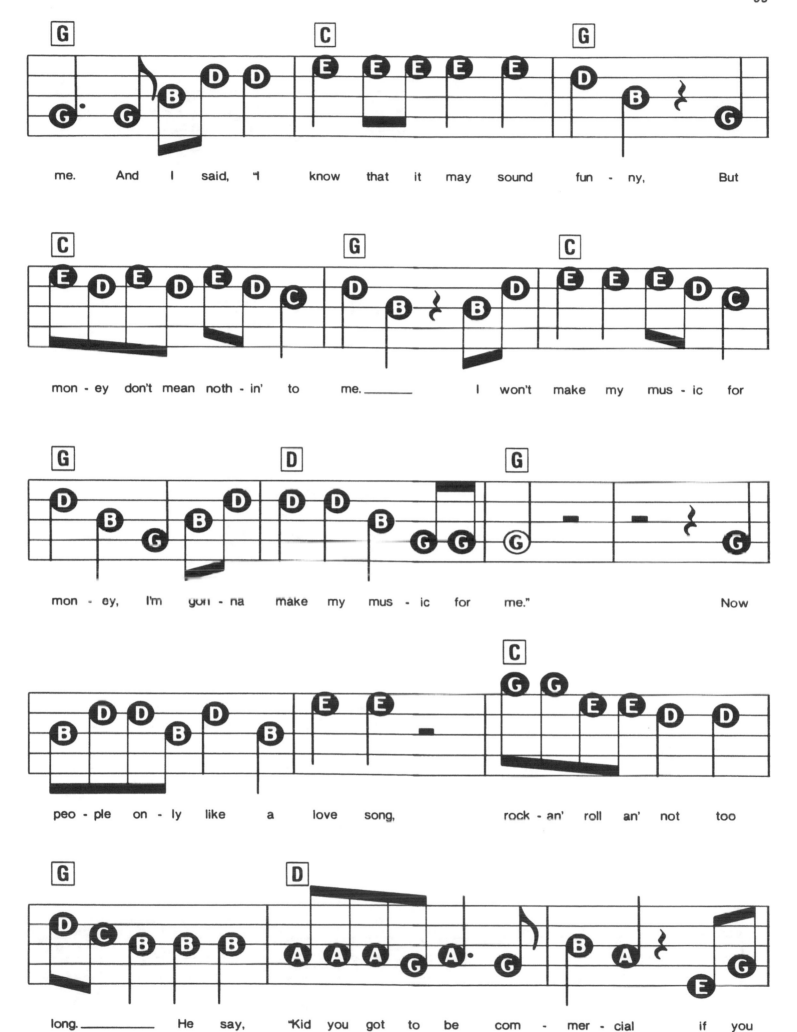

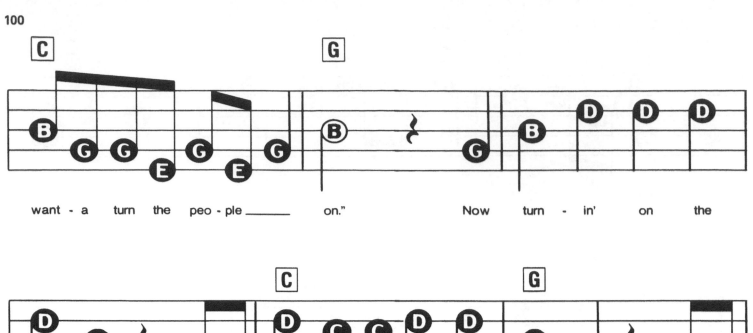

want-a turn the peo-ple _____ on." Now turn-in' on the

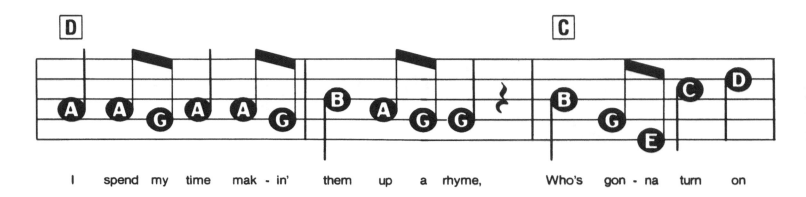

peo - ple What a beau - ti - ful place to be, _____ But if

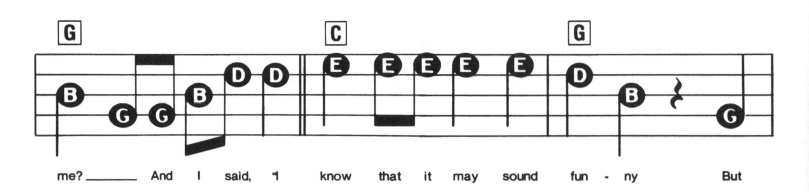

I spend my time mak - in' them up a rhyme, Who's gon - na turn on

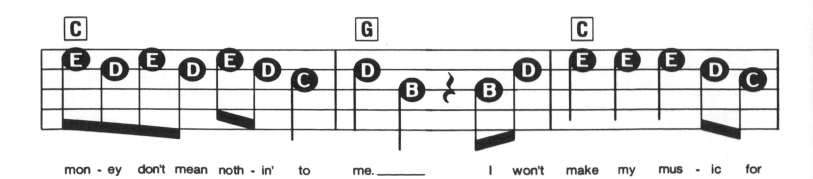

me? _____ And I said, "I know that it may sound fun - ny But

C   G   C

mon - ey don't mean noth - in' to me. _____ I won't make my mus - ic for

101

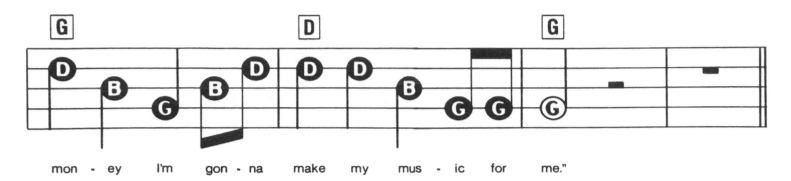

mon - ey I'm gon - na make my mus - ic for me."

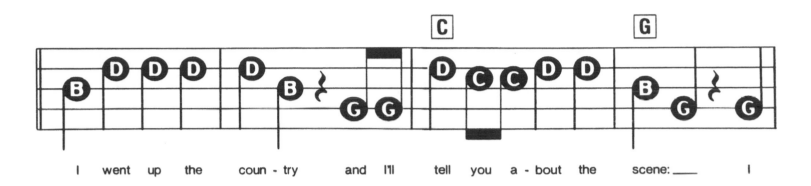

I went up the coun - try and I'll tell you a - bout the scene: ___ I

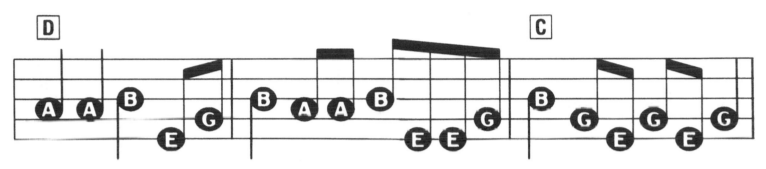

found a place with much charm and much grace that was - n't touched by the mus - ic ma -

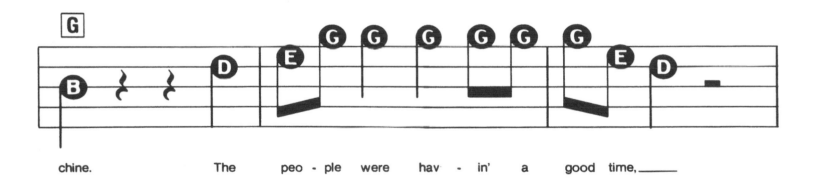

chine. The peo - ple were hav - in' a good time, ___

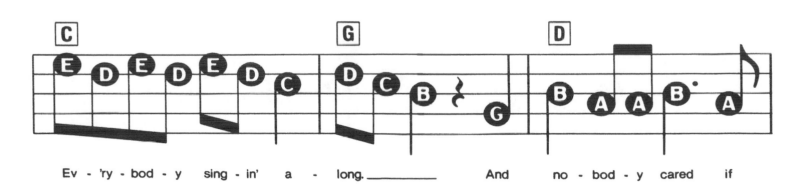

Ev - 'ry - bod - y sing - in' a - long. ___ And no - bod - y cared if

102

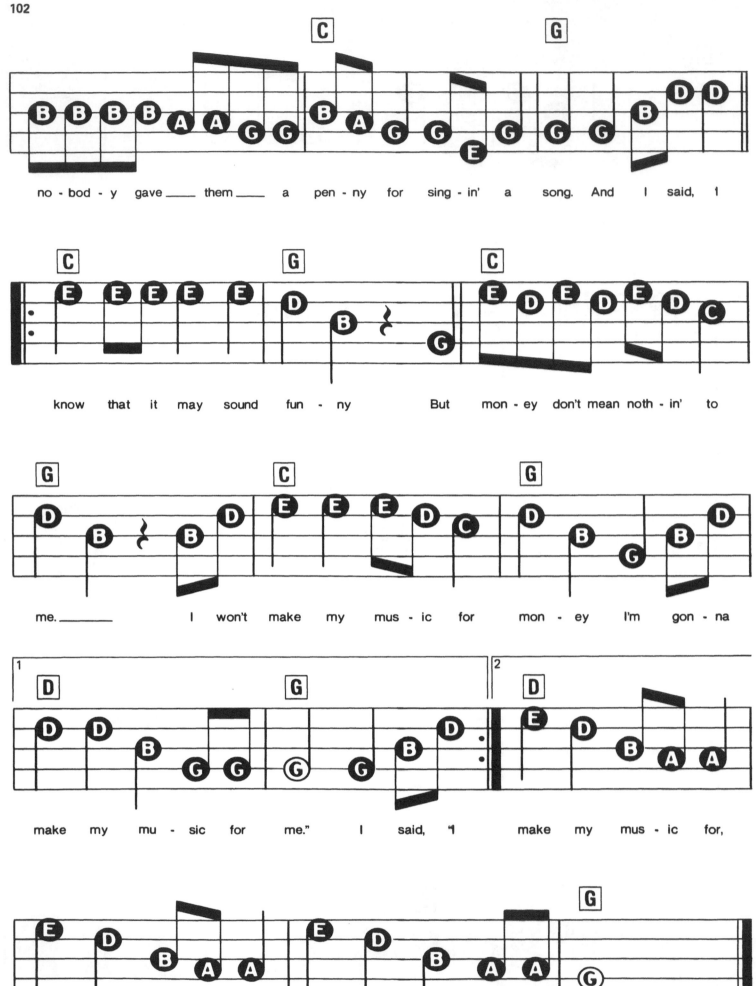

There's An Old Man In Our Town

Registration 1
Rhythm: Ballad

Words and Music by Kenny Rogers

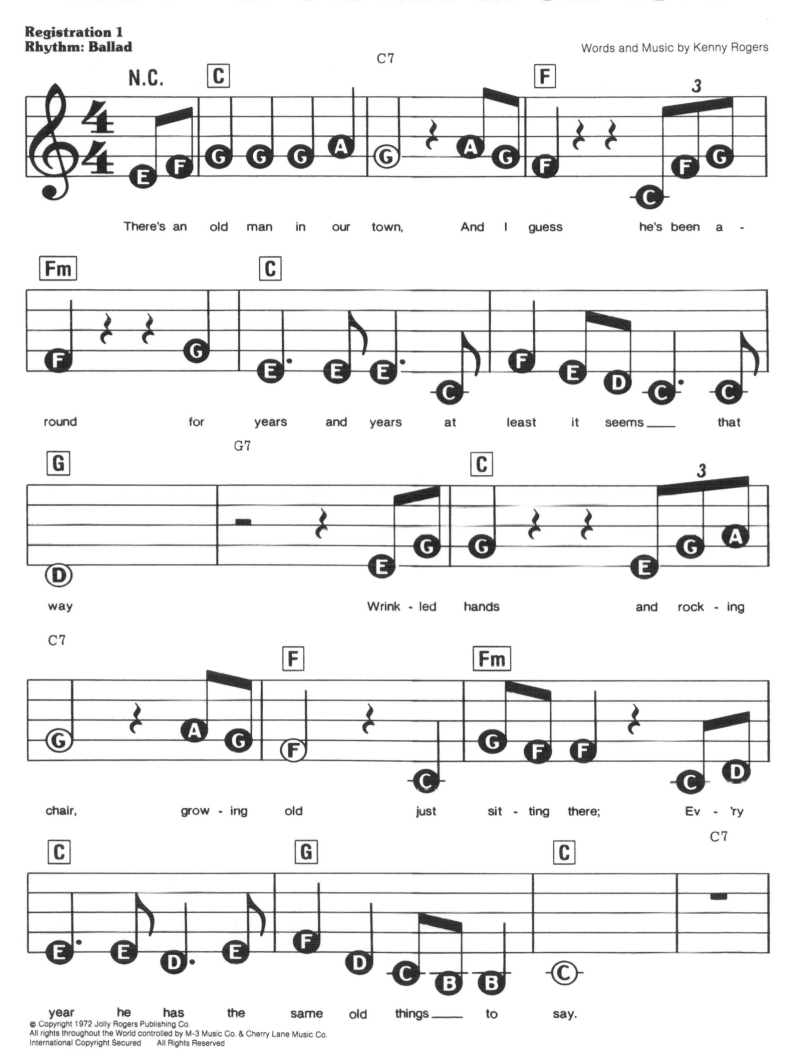

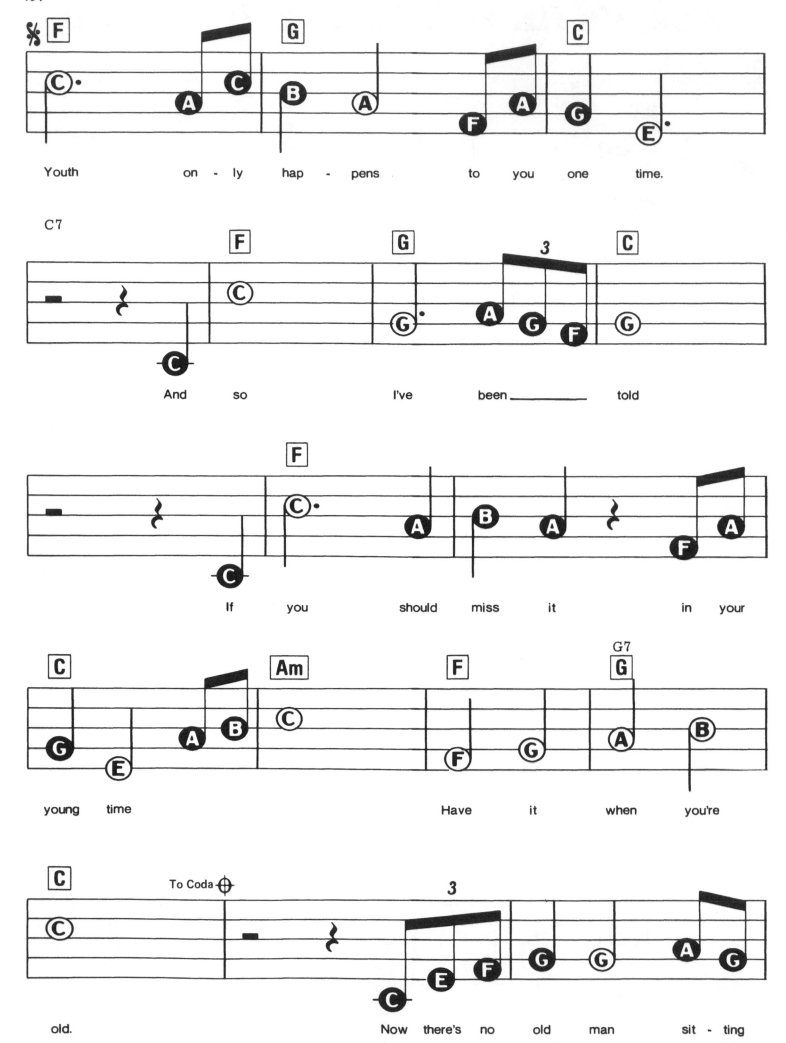

Daytime Friends

Registration 2
Rhythm: March

Words and Music by Ben Peters

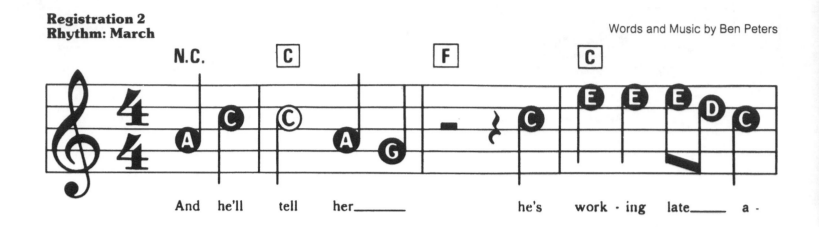

And he'll tell her_____ he's work-ing late_____ a-

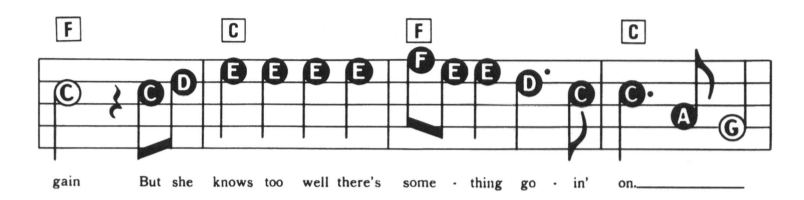

gain   But she knows too well there's some-thing go-in' on._____

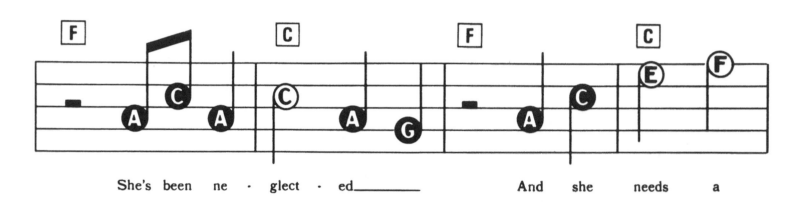

She's been ne-glect-ed_____   And she needs a

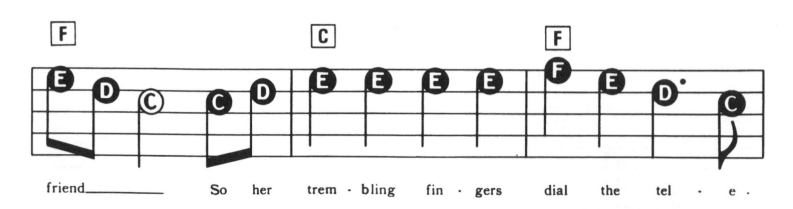

friend_____   So her trem-bling fin-gers dial the tel-e-

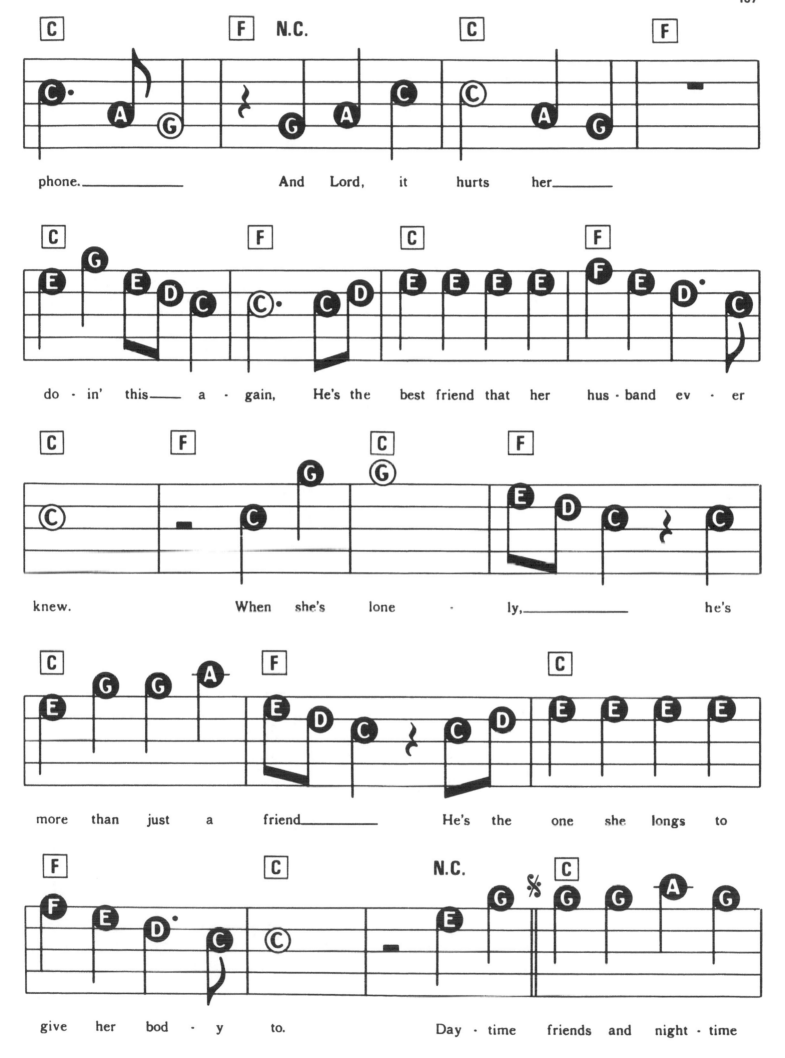

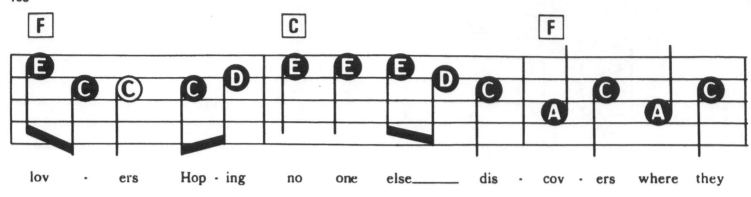

lov - ers Hop - ing no one else___ dis - cov - ers where they

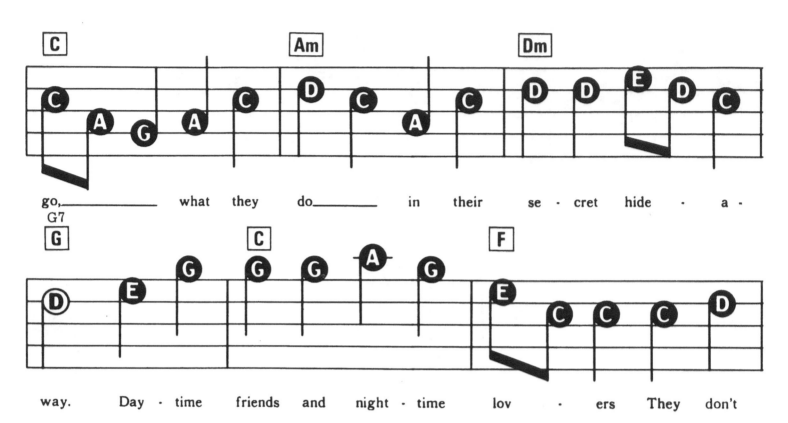

go,___ what they do___ in their se - cret hide - a -

way. Day - time friends and night - time lov - ers They don't

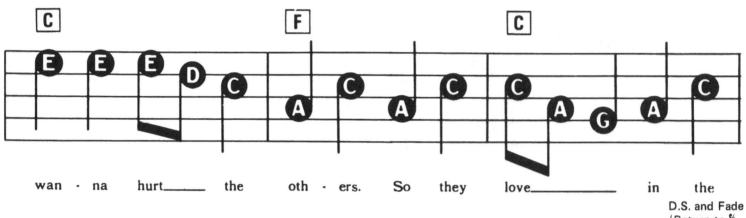

wan - na hurt___ the oth - ers. So they love___ in the

D.S. and Fade
(Return to 𝄋
and Fade)

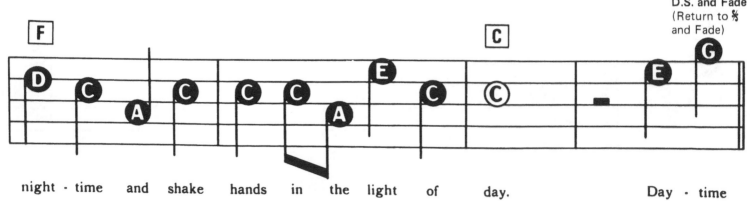

night - time and shake hands in the light of day. Day - time

You Decorated My Life

Words and Music by
Bob Morrison and Debbie Hupp

Registration 1
Rhythm: Ballad or Fox Trot

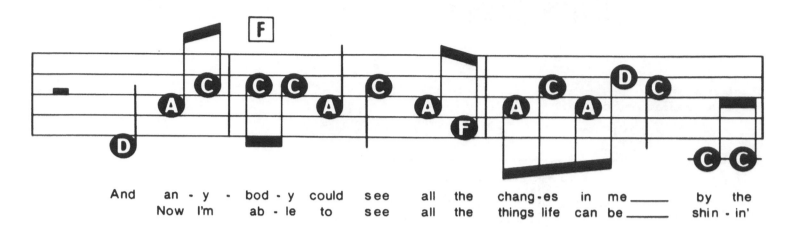

And   an - y - bod - y   could   see   all   the   chang - es   in   me_____   by   the
Now   I'm   ab - le   to   see   all   the   things life   can   be_____   shin - in'

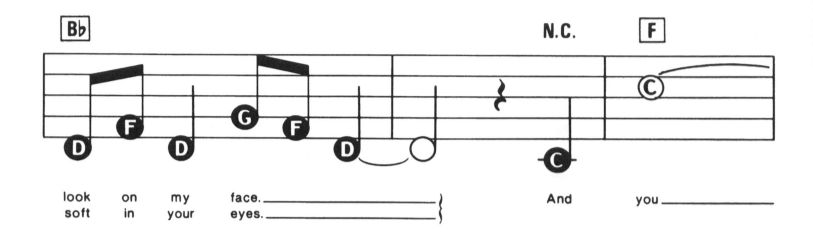

look   on   my   face._____   And   you_____
soft   in   your   eyes._____

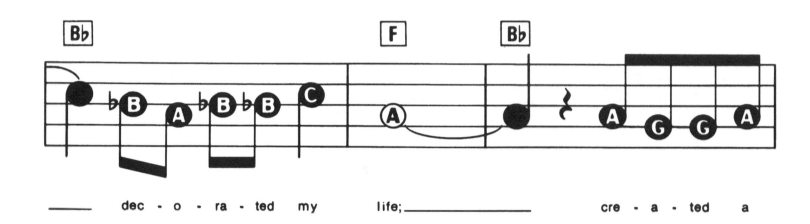

_____   dec - o - ra - ted   my   life;_____   cre - a - ted   a

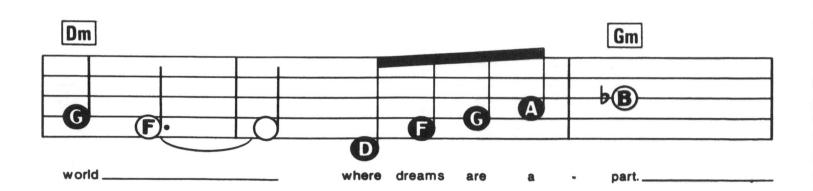

world_____   where   dreams   are   a - part._____

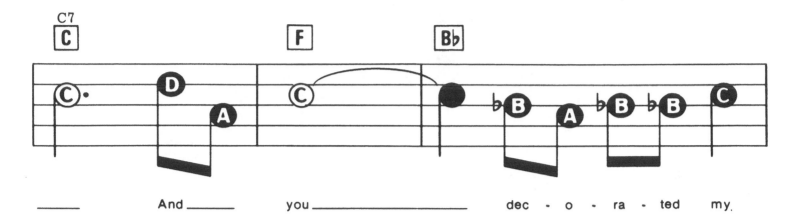

And _____ you _____ dec - o - ra - ted my

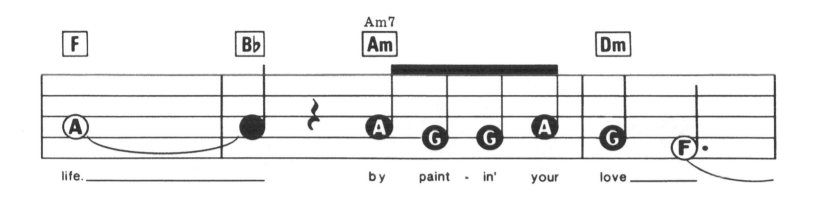

life. _____ by paint - in' your love _____

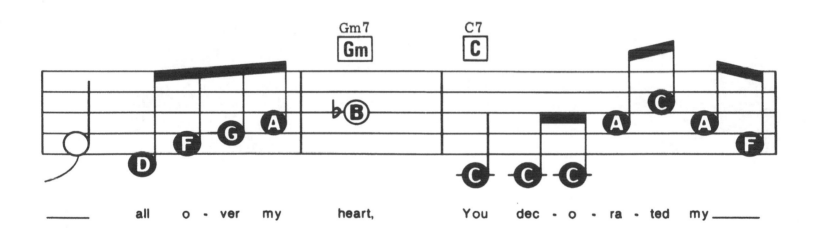

_____ all o - ver my heart, You dec - o - ra - ted my _____

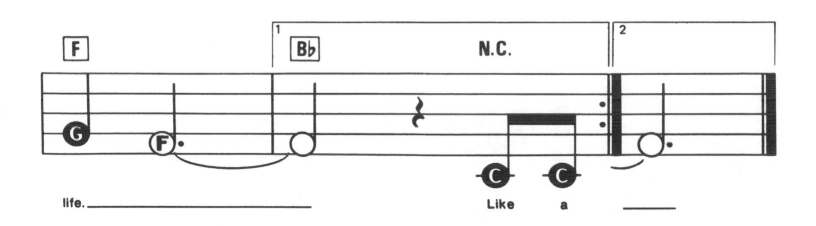

life. _____ Like a _____